Engaging with Engagement

Engaging with Engagement: Analysing the Formation of Promises, Contracts and Voluntary Obligations in Scots Law

Jonathan Brown

ANTHEM PRESS

Anthem Press
An imprint of Wimbledon Publishing Company
www.anthempress.com

This edition first published in UK and USA 2026
by ANTHEM PRESS
75–76 Blackfriars Road, London SE1 8HA, UK
or PO Box 9779, London SW19 7ZG, UK
and
244 Madison Ave #116, New York, NY 10016, USA

British Library Cataloguing-in-Publication Data
A catalogue record for this book is available from the British Library.

Library of Congress Cataloging-in-Publication Data: 2025947724
A catalog record for this book has been requested.

ISBN-13: 978-1-83999-651-1 (Hbk)
ISBN-10: 1-83999-651-X (Hbk)

This title is also available as an eBook.

CONTENTS

TABLE OF CASES

Scotland

England and Wales

Privy Council

South Africa

TABLE OF LEGISLATION

Acts of the Parliament of Scotland (pre-1707)

Acts of the Scottish Parliament (1999–Present)

Acts of the Parliament of the United Kingdom of Great Britain and Ireland

Acts of the Parliament of the United Kingdom of Great Britain and Northern Ireland

ACKNOWLEDGEMENTS

This short book owes its life in its present form to a suggestion by Professor Jane Mair of the University of Glasgow, who happens to presently be the editor of the *Juridical Review*. Initially, I approached Jane with a collection of disjointed thoughts so as to obtain her view as to whether or not the *Juridical* might consider publishing them (once suitably arranged) in a multi-part article series. Though she was supportive and found the jumbled piece that I sent through to be interesting, she suggested that it might be better if the thoughts were developed into a short book. So it proved to be so. With Professor Mair's encouragement – and for that matter, the encouragement of my excellent colleagues Professor Adelyn Wilson and Professor Douglas Brodie, to whom I am also very much indebted and who both also expressed the view that I had developed the germ of a book rather than a mere collection of articles – I contacted Professor Russell Sandberg, the present editor of the Anthem Studies in Law Reform Series. Professor Sandberg proved most supportive of the proposal to work my thoughts into this short book also and – thus – the present work, at least in concept, was born. In practice, it's taken some time for the work to go through the rigours of peer review and so I owe a sincere word of thanks to the anonymous peer-reviewers for their thorough and detailed comments on the manuscript and I also owe thanks to the team at Anthem Press – particularly Golda Merline and Jebaslin Hephzibah – for guiding the work from manuscript to press. A word of thanks should be voiced, too, to my wonderful colleagues at the University of Strathclyde: I am extremely fortunate to work in such a supportive environment with so many learned, enthusiastic and, for that matter, fun colleagues. In that vein, a particular word of thanks should go to Mr Roddy Cairns, my fellow teacher of the Scots law of voluntary obligations at Strathclyde. I count myself lucky that I work alongside one who cares about the future of our discipline and profession as he.

I owe a sincere word of thanks to my good friend and erstwhile office-mate, Dr Leslie Dodd, for his ever-engaging conversations about all aspects of Scots private law, legal history and general culture. Professors Adelyn Wilson and Douglas Brodie again deserve a second mention, as they have done much to support me in my career development as an academic and, more particularly, to offer encouragement in the writing of this book. Above all, however, I owe – as ever – a sincere, deep and extremely heartfelt word of thanks to my wife, Dr Jennifer Mattschey, whom I love more than words can adequately express. If not for her indulgence of my predilection for researching topics which she simply could not care less about, this book would not exist. Thank you Jenn.

Dr Jonathan Brown
19/09/2025

INTRODUCTION: PROPOSALS TO REFORM SCOTS 'CONTRACT LAW' AND THE ONCOMING STORM

In 2018, the Scottish Law Commission (SLC) proposed that the law pertaining to the formation of voluntary obligations should be significantly reformed. Under the aegis of a review of Scots 'contract law', a draft bill was produced[1] and in 2021 the Scottish government's proposed programme for the 2021–2026 Parliament set out a commitment to 'a longer-term programme of implementation of Scottish Law Commission Reports'.[2] This led, in July 2024, to a consultation concerning the possible implementation of the SLC's recommendation(s) and the prospective enactment of the draft bill, or at least something akin to it in an amended (to a greater or lesser extent) form.[3] Given the SLC's recent success in seeing the implementation of reforms to areas such as defamation,[4] moveable transactions[5] and trusts[6] (among other things) in recent years, it may be thought that the prevailing winds of change will see this proposed reform sail through also. This short book, however, seeks to make the case that if such were to eventuate, considerable harm would be done to the fabric, framework and intellectual coherence of Scots private law as a whole. In a sense, it is a work of 'anti-law reform' advocacy. Perhaps this is unusual for a contribution to the Anthem Studies in Law Reform Series, but nonetheless it is thought that advocates for change in the law – particularly in private law – must be made aware of the intellectual inheritance that may be squandered if centuries of tradition are indeed to be swept away, essentially overnight, by legislative fiat.

Fundamentally, by consulting on the subject of 'contract law' in and of itself, the SLC made a grave category error in failing to recognise the overarching intellectual coherence and unity of 'obligations', as a taxonomical topic, within Scottish jurisprudence. Unlike in most English-speaking jurisdictions (which tend to be, but are not exclusively,[7] big-C 'Common law' jurisdictions – that is, their legal framework emerged out of the learned tradition of the English Common law as developed in the Royal Courts of that

Kingdom)[8] Scotland does not, properly speaking, have a law of 'contract' or 'contracts' but rather a broad law of voluntary obligations of which 'contracts' form but a part[9] (albeit, clearly, the most significantly recognisable, and commonly litigated, part).[10] The intellectual contribution of the great Scots jurist James Dalrymple, the 1st Viscount Stair, did not merely ensure that Scots law was in a fit state to survive Scotland's political union with England in 1707,[11] though unquestionably it did contribute to the eventuation of this outcome.[12] In addition to ensuring the endurance of Scots law as an independent framework within a predominantly Common law-dominated political union (to say nothing of Empire/Commonwealth), Stair's philosophical approach to the rationalisation of law was also radical, in some respects arguably timeless,[13] and led to the creation of a system of jurisprudence essentially unique to Scotland as compared with even principally Civil law – by which is meant Roman law-derived[14] – jurisdictions.[15]

While other systems (Civil and Common alike) may divide 'events' which give rise to 'personal rights' between those which arise from agreement, those which arise from wrongdoing and those which arise from nebulous 'other causes',[16] Scots law, since at least the seventeenth century, has recognised an essential divide between *obligationes ex voluntate* (those which arise 'by will') and those which are imposed *ex lege* ('by law').[17] It remains the case, therefore, that any scholar who wishes to understand the theory of Scots 'contract law' must start with Stair,[18] but much more pertinently such scholars must also appreciate the fact that for Stair 'contract law' is not an independent, primary topic sequestered to its own corner of the legal system. Rather, 'contracts' exist, in fact, as a mere sub-category of a broader descriptive taxonomical class.[19] That the SLC chose to consider the 'law of contract' in isolation is consequently problematic and indeed – it is here thought – led to proposals which, if enacted, would lead to the eventuation of deleterious consequences for Scots law as a rational and ordered system and may even threaten the ongoing viability of Scotland's distinct legal framework. As the late, great jurist Peter Birks observed, though 'some Scots lawyers take the view that the identity of Scots law consists in the content of particular rules' this is not in fact – and never has been – so. 'The true difference [between Scots and English jurisprudence] consist[s] in the [Scots'] commitment to the institutional scheme, or, in other words, to a more systematic approach. Scots law might have claimed [and still might yet claim] a higher rationality, because concern to arrange the law intelligibly is the clearest manifestation of a determined rationality.'[20]

Indeed, perhaps ironically, it is because of the traditional Scottish commitment to 'determined rationality' and the conceptual ordering of 'law' as an intellectual subject of study, that the Westminster Parliament was, in the mid-1960s, initially reluctant to expand the remit of the Law Commissions Act 1965 to apply to Scotland.[21] In fact, the prevailing view at the time, prior to the eventual 'tacking on' of Scotland to an Act principally driven by 'English circumstances and English pressures',[22] was that 'Scots law was [...] in less need of reform than English law, due to its Civilian heritage and restatement of the civil law by Stair in the Seventeenth Century'.[23] While, then, there were some in Parliament who would preach 'legitimate pride in the superiority of English law over Roman law and other foreign systems',[24] it was even then recognised by the same such figures that this attitude 'often blinded [English lawyers] to the experience that can sometimes be derived from developments in the Commonwealth and other countries, to say nothing of Scotland'.[25] Stair's inheritance – preached as so enduring and vital, particularly in respect of the law pertaining to voluntary obligations[26] – is one which can and, it is argued in this volume, ought to be made use of in preference to fractured and disjointed legislative reform.

Rather than presenting a taxonomy that is 'stuck in the Seventeenth Century',[27] Stair produced an *opus* that is 'so well digested in all its parts, so liberal in principle, so good in arrangement, so distinguished for sound judgment and excellent adaptation to the business and concerns of men that it would seem almost beyond the age in which it was written'.[28] Teachers, scholars and, indeed, even prospective reformers of Scots law ought, consequently, to pay due regard to Stair's intellectual efforts in order to ascertain what the law is and ought to be according to first principles, with a view to rationalising and explaining the operation of the law as it stands. To that end, then, this present volume provides a re-analysis and re-appraisal of Stair's taxonomy of voluntary obligations and the formation thereof, as a means of making the case that the Scottish Parliament should not rush to reform the law of 'contract formation' as it stands, even though it has been urged to do so by the learned law commissioners. The purpose of the piece is inescapably polemical, yet it is thought that the scholarship underpinning the argument is sound and merits serious consideration by prospective law reformers, Parliamentarians and lawyers. To wit, the book considers, in detail, one particular aspect of the proposals of the SLC – a recommendation which, in fact, was so uncontroversial at the time of the SLC's report that it attracted unanimous support from the respondents to the SLC's consultation – the planned abolishment of the 'postal acceptance rule'.[29] The nature of this rule has hitherto been conceptualised by academics – and by some (though certainly not all judges)[30] – as being essentially the same in this jurisdiction as it is in the Common law world.[31] That is to say, it is generally thought that the 'postal acceptance rule' exists as an exceptional quirk of the Victorian age which should – ideally – be excised from the law as 'out of keeping' with modern life in the twenty-first century.[32]

This book seeks to establish that notwithstanding the prevailing orthodoxy, the conceptualisation of the 'postal acceptance rule' as an exception is in Scots law – whatever the position may be in the Common law world – fundamentally incorrect. Instead of being in any way 'exceptional', the 'postal acceptance rule' is in fact nothing more than a manifestation of the ordinary rules pertaining to the creation of voluntary obligations in this jurisdiction.[33] The mistaken belief that the Scots 'postal acceptance rule' is in any way exceptional has arisen from a culture which has come to regard Scotland as being in possession, simply, of a 'law of contract' akin to the English equivalent,[34] when that is not in fact the case.[35] By considering Viscount Stair's approach to the formation of voluntary obligations, it can be seen that – rather than being an odd Victorian exception to some general rule – the operation of the 'postal acceptance rule' in Scots law is in fact a manifestation of the general rule of Scots law that voluntary obligations are created by overt acts of engagement on the part of prospective obligants. This, clearly, has consequences for the question of formation of contract in Scotland: rather than seeking to limit the operation of the 'postal rule', or abolish it altogether,[36] it would appear that its precepts should be taken to apply more generally to analyses of 'offer + acceptance' contract formation in this jurisdiction, with resultant consequences for issues such as contracts concluded via email, text messaging (or other forms of both instantaneous and non-instantaneous messaging) and so on. Such, it is submitted, is indicative of the timelessness of Stair's intellectual contribution.

In other words, by examining the philosophical approach to the formation of 'voluntary obligations' taken by Stair – who, as an 'Institutional writer', wrote manifestly with a principally pedagogical (or rather andragogical) purpose in mind[37] – a flexible framework which is capable of ready adaptation to novel (including unforeseen and presently unforeseeable) situations can be worked out by application of reason. While, indeed, it is the case that Scotland is a small jurisdiction which does not produce a large amount of case law, and – if case law is seen to be the principal driver of (small 'c') common law development – this inevitably does suggest that there is perhaps not enough to 'enable the law to keep moving with the times',[38] it must nevertheless be borne in mind that Scotland is not a big 'C' Common law jurisdiction exclusively reliant on incremental development of small 'c' common law through the courts.[39] Consequently, case law cannot and should not be viewed as the principal source of common (or customary) legal development in this jurisdiction: within the Scottish tradition there has been a long history of using the works of learned treatise writers to supplement, develop and guide the evolution of legal change.[40] As Blackie and Whitty observed in an essay written in honour of Professor W. A. Wilson, throughout the twentieth century 'textbooks [were] generally cited more frequently [in Scotland] than in England [and] simply counting the number of cases in which reference made to [such] source[s] does not [...] reveal the full picture. [...] in the Scots cases the texts are repeatedly cited for major points of law [...] referred to as "authorities" [...] [with the net effect that] the way that the courts use writings is a distinctive feature of our case law [and] not a surprising one in a small legal system'.[41] This phenomenon, it is here submitted, is quite distinct from the well-known and anomalous treatment of a *numerus clausus* of so-called 'Institutional writers' as positive sources of authority, in and of themselves, within the Scottish system.[42]

Bearing this in mind, it is notable that though Scotland continues to produce comparatively little (reported) case law, the publication of learned writings on Scots law has multiplied almost exponentially.[43] Through long-standing initiatives such as the Scottish Universities Law Institute,[44] and more recent endowments and support from organisations such as the Edinburgh Legal Education Trust,[45] there exists a flourishing ecosystem to facilitate the development and publication of excellent Scottish legal scholarship and indeed, if it may be ventured that 'probably more has been written on [Scots] enrichment law in the past 30 years than in the previous 300 years',[46] to take but one topic, no small part of the reason for this is that more monograph-length texts (to say nothing of shorter articles and other contributions), from a more diverse cast of authors, have been written on Scots private law generally, in that same period, than at any other time in history. Indeed, as Hogg recently observed, much of the scholarship that has considered what are, essentially, basic concepts within Scottish jurisprudence has been outstanding and made significant, original contributions to knowledge.[47] The 'theoretical' authority of these hypothetical *explananda* of Scots jurisprudence, to use that Latin term in the sense employed by Michelon,[48] has the potential to allow for a more rational, sensible and – perhaps seemingly counterintuitively – accessible evolution of the law than bespoke, fragmented and piecemeal legislation. After all, there is a reason that Scots private (and indeed criminal) law remained in such a surprisingly healthy state despite the jurisdiction's functional lack of an interested legislature for nigh-on some three hundred years.

There is however, ostensibly, something of an irony in arguing that Stair's intellectual schema should be thought preferable to legislative intervention, given the (great) man's own view that 'law must derive from a lawgiver, not from a group of legal experts'.[49] Nonetheless, it was also Stair who observed that

> 'the nations are more happy whose laws have been entered by long custom, wrung out from their debates on particular cases, until it came to the consistence of a fixed and known custom. For thereby the conveniences and inconveniences thereof through a long tract of times are experimentally seen. So that which is found in some cases convenient, if in other cases it be found inconvenient, it proves abortive in the womb of time, before it attain the maturity of a law. But in statutes the lawgiver must at once balances the conveniences and inconveniences; wherein he may and often doth fall short'.[50]

In effect, then, though this account 'depends on a view of the world [...] and of the nature of law which is now wholly out of fashion',[51] given that it behoves scholars of law to be intellectuals rather than dedicated followers of fashion,[52] Stair's observations about the limitations of legislation remain germane. Particularly so when the words of the Roman jurist Ulpian echo in the 1707 Treaty of Union,[53] and so within the constitutional place of Scotland in the United Kingdom itself:[54] 'new statutes, concerning things, should be of evident utility, since to depart from what has been thought lawfully right for a long time must be seen to be fair'.[55]

Stair's taxonomy and intellectual framework concerning obligations have been thought right by lawyers and scholars for a long time indeed. As such, it is hoped that the Scottish Parliament and SLC might, following the words of caution contained in this book, take pause to consider whether or not the enactment of a bespoke statutory framework concerning so narrow a topic as 'formation of contract' is, in fact, for the 'evident utility' of the people of Scotland. Here, it is suggested, there is no such utility, still less 'evident' utility; the status quo itself might not be ideal, but the development of law outwith the confines of rigid statute, in so prosaic a matter such as this, would appear better able to serve the needs of a changing society. To support this thesis, the present book is divided into three chapters: the first sets out the intellectual framework of 'obligations' pioneered by Stair, noting that core to this framework is his conception of 'will' and, particularly, 'engagement'. Recognising that the typology of Stair's 'acts of the will' is readily capable of explaining phenomena such as 'invitations to treat' and the 'offer + acceptance = contract' analysis within so-called 'contract law', the chapter further notes that Stair's framework in fact goes further and can be employed as a useful heuristic for questions concerning the formation of unilateral promises, as well as in fact testaments and trusts, also. Accordingly, this chapter concludes by considering the fact that the scale of Stair's intellectual achievement is often understated, even by otherwise excellent scholars. Rather than providing a taxonomy dividing 'obligations arising by agreement and obligations imposed without regard to agreement',[56] as some have simplistically contended, in fact it must be recognised that by virtue of Stair's taxonomy the notion 'agreement' does not play the definitive role in respect of obligations-formation in the Scottish legal system that it does in other systems, of whatever 'legal family'.

Against this background, the second chapter comparatively considers the so-called 'postal acceptance rule' within the context of Scots jurisprudence. Recognising that – in spite of the SLC's contention to the contrary[57] – the Scottish 'rule' was not received from the courts of England and Wales, the chapter demonstrates that by logically applying the intellectual framework pioneered by Stair, and later adopted by subsequent 'Institutional writers' such as George Joseph Bell,[58] it can be demonstrated that there is in fact no bespoke 'postal exception' in Scots law, as the general rule of obligation-formation in that jurisdiction holds that communication of the act of engagement to any beneficiary thereof is immaterial. This, it is submitted, ought to have significant consequences for (*inter alia*) attempts to form contracts via modern means of communication such as text messages, emails, instant messaging services et cetera. While, then, the potential for the development of a novel and useful legal framework which can flexibly accommodate technological advances (latently) subsists in Scots law, the chapter concludes that the SLC's proposals to brutally excise 'any rule of law whereby, in relation to the formation of a contract, an acceptance sent by means of a postal service takes effect when posted' would, it is feared, inevitably stymy this latent flexibility.

Accordingly, in recognition of such, the third chapter explores the 'double-bind' that the Scottish Law Commissioners find themselves in, by virtue of their essentially conflicting statutory duties. Though it has been recognised since at least the time of Cicero that a proliferation of statutes leads only to the proliferation of injustice,[59] the Law Commissioners are nonetheless simultaneously bound to codify the law while simultaneously simplifying it.[60] In the absence of Continental-style codification of 'private law' as a holistic topic, an alleged impossibility given the present, fundamentally Common law, methodology applied in respect of statutory interpretation and construction in Scotland today,[61] simplification through codification is an impossibility: instead of conceptual unity, there can be only piecemeal statute. This state of affairs is, it is submitted, unsatisfactory, particularly given Professor Watson's warning that the wheels of law reform (particularly private law reform) move very slowly indeed.[62] As his illuminating studies *Failures of the Legal Imagination*[63] and *Society and Legal Change*,[64] as well as the practical thesis advanced in *Slave Law in the Americas*, make plain, almost all societies have an absurdly high tolerance for inappropriate and unsatisfactory law.[65] Consequently, rather than optimistically supposing, as Professor MacQueen does, that if piecemeal legislative reform 'turn[s] out to be ill, [such] could then be reformed with better understanding of what the problems for solution are',[66] it would seem rather that if a legislative Act such as the enactment of the proposed Contract (Formation) (Scotland) Bill were to occur, then the new legal order created by it would be likely to endure and subsist no matter what harms happened to be inflicted upon Scots law by its passing.

The third chapter, then, considers the pressures that the SLC are under to enact piecemeal statutes and explores the drawbacks of such in the round: more particularly, however, the chapter also explores the purported rationale(s) for the abrogation of the so-called 'postal acceptance rule' in Scotland and seeks to establish that the purported 'difficulties' with the rule can in fact be elided without statutory intervention. Accordingly, the chapter concludes by suggesting that notwithstanding their overarching duty to concern themselves with the 'codification' of the law, Law Commissioners should in fact exercise restraint where fundamental topics of law are concerned, and indeed should seek to encourage – where possible – the conceptual unity of law as an intellectual and rational discipline. In Scotland, Stair's *Institutions* provides a useful, and indeed nigh-timeless, model for the ongoing 'systematic development' of the law. Rather than breaking this system of institutional order apart, it rather behoves law reformers, scholars and jurisprudents to uphold the legal system as just that: a rational normative order which can usefully and predictably order the operation of harmonious human intercourse.

Notes

1 Scottish Law Commission, *Report on Review of Contract Law: Formation, Interpretation, Remedies for Breach, and Penalty Clauses*, March 2018 (Scot. Law Com. No.252), Appendix A.

2 Scottish Government, *A Fairer, Greener Scotland Programme for Government 2021–22* (OGL, 2021), 119.

3 Justice Directorate, *Scottish Law Commission – Contract Law Review Report: Consultation* (OGL, 2024).

4 See the Defamation and Malicious Publications (Scotland) Act 2021.

5 See the Moveable Transactions (Scotland) Act 2023.

6 See the Trusts and Succession (Scotland) Act 2024.

7 Consider, for example, South Africa and the State of Louisiana, both of which are regarded as archetypal 'mixed' jurisdictions: See, generally, Vernon V. Palmer (ed.), *Mixed Jurisdictions Worldwide* (2nd edn) (Cambridge University Press, 2012).

8 See Sir Frederick Pollock and Frederic W. Maitland, *The History of English Law Before the Time of Edward I* (2nd edn) (Cambridge University Press, 1898), 184.

9 Of course, while 'contract does not exhaust the category of voluntarily undertaken obligations' in Scotland and 'Scots law recognises a separate and distinct type of voluntary obligation, usually referred to as promise or unilateral obligation', 'paradoxically, most discussion of unilateral obligations is to be found in books

headed "Contract" or the like': Gerry Maher, *Unilateral Obligations and International Private Law*, (2002) Jur. Rev. 317, at 317.

10 In this, the present author fundamentally disagrees with Gloag, who preferred the language of 'contract law' over that of 'voluntary obligations' (despite acknowledging that the former was not 'sufficiently comprehensive for his purpose') claiming that 'obligations by one party only [are] relatively unimportant': William M. Gloag, *The Law of Contract* (2nd edn) (Caledonian Books, 1985), at 1. Gloag's bold statement has, ultimately, proven to be inescapably wrong, as the growing literature and case law concerned with unilateral promise plainly demonstrates: see, e.g., the discussion in Hector L. MacQueen, *My Word Is My Bond: Unilateral Promises Once More*, [2019] SLT (News) 103.

11 See John W.G. Blackie, 'Stair's Later Reputation as a Jurist' in David M. Walker (ed.), *Stair Tercentenary Studies* (Stair Society, 1981), 227, though it was not ever thus: 'if there is something common to all present-day attitudes [...] it is that Stair's work is the foundation of all useful discussion of Scottish private law. In certain cases it can even appear that later law is simply a footnote, and a misleading one at that. Stair may be presented as law before the fall.' While it may be countered that, ultimately, 'Romantic nationalism [...] seems the easiest explanation for the emergence of Stair as the true guide to what is peculiarly Scots and peculiarly excellent in the law', such does not detract from the ultimate utility of Stair's organising theory, particularly where the law of obligations is concerned.

12 'In some measure, this assessment relies on hindsight': Andreas Rahmatian, *The Role of Institutional Writers in Scots Law*, [2018] Jur. Rev. 42, 44.

13 Consider, for instance, the reflections of Lord Rodger of Earlsferry on Joe Thomson, *Scots Private Law* (W. Green, 2006): the characters used, therein, to illustratively demonstrate the operation of the law 'lead relatively humdrum lives [...] they have to confront problems which could have featured in classical Roman law, or in Scots law at any time during its history'. Though 'some of the examples have a rather old-fashioned air', 'there is, of course, much to be said for using timeless and simple examples of transactions between individuals. They concentrate the mind on the essential legal questions. They are also [...] the kinds of apparently mundane problems which might crop up in a citizen's advice bureau': Lord Rodger of Earlsferry, *'Only Connect'*, [2007] Jur. Rev. 164, at 166–167. In like vein, Stair's philosophical approach to the formation of voluntary obligations is capable, through undergraduate (and arguably sub-undergraduate) intellectual effort, of ready application to novel situations which Stair himself could not have foreseen or imagined.

14 See, generally, Arthur T. Von Mehren, Hao Jiang and James R. Gordley, *An Introduction to the Comparative Study of Private Law: Readings, Cases, Materials* (2nd edn) (Cambridge University Press, 2021), 3.

15 It is sometimes forgotten, to the discredit of Scots jurists generally, that some Scots law – and 'not a little' at that – is homegrown: George L. Gretton, 'The Rational and the National: Thomas Broun Smith' in Elspeth C. Reid and David L. Carey Miller, *A Mixed Legal System in Transition: T. B. Smith and the Progress of Scots Law* (Edinburgh University Press, 2005), 33.

16 See the discussion in Peter Birks, 'Definition and Division: A Meditation on *Institutes* 3.13' in Peter Birks (ed.), *The Classification of Obligations* (Clarendon Press, 1997), 17–27.

17 Stair, *Institutions of the Law of Scotland* (Andrew Anderson, 1681; 2nd edn, 1693), I, 10, 1.

18 Martin Hogg, *Perspectives on Contract Theory from a Mixed Jurisdiction*, [2009] OJLS 643, 648.

19 Indeed, the term 'obligation' appeared 'in the Roman sense of a *juris vinculum* binding two persons' within *Regiam Majestatem*: See Gerhard Lubbe, 'Formation of Contract' in Kenneth Reid and Reinhard Zimmermann, *A History of Private Law in Scotland: Volume 2: Obligations* (Oxford University Press, 2000), 6.

20 Peter Birks, 'More Logic and Less Experience: The Difference Between Scots and English Law' in David L. Carey Miller and Reinhard Zimmermann, *The Civilian Tradition and Scots Law: Aberdeen Quincentenary Essays* (Duncker and Humblot, 1997) 174.

21 Lord Chancellor Gairdner's initial plan had been to 'start with England', although ultimately 'Scotsmen know a good thing when they see one and they were not going to be left out' – HL Debate 1 April 1965, col 1156 – with Professor T.B. Smith being credited in large part with causing the addition of the relevant Scots provisions – Lord Hunter, *Thomas Broun Smith 1915–1988*, [1992] Proceedings of the British Academy 455, at 466 – and the work of securing a separate Scottish Commission being largely effected by then-Secretary of State for Scotland Willie Ross: George L. Gretton, *On Law Commissioning*, [2013] Edin. L. R. 119, 123.

22 Shona Wilson-Stark, *The Longer You Can Look Back, The Further You Can Look Forward: The Origins of the Scottish Law Commission*, [2014] Edin. L. R. 59, 65.

23 Ibid.

24 HC Debate 8 February 1965 col 55, *per* Sir E. Fletcher.

25 Ibid.

26 Hogg, *Perspectives*, 648; *Cawdor v. Cawdor*, 2007 SC 285, para.15; *Regus Maxim Ltd. v. Bank of Scotland Plc* [2013] CSIH 12.

27 This aphorism was the redoubt of reformers who sought to 'modernise' the law pertaining to *ius quaesitum tertio*: See Douglas Mathie, *Third Party Rights – Scots Law Stuck in the 17th Century*, August 2010, accessible at https://brodiestechblog.wordpress.com/2010/08/26/third-party-rights-%E2%80%93-scots-law-stuck-in-the17thcentury/.

28 George Joseph Bell, *Commentaries on the Laws of Scotland and on the Principles of Mercantile Jurisprudence*, Volume I (5th edn) (Blackwood, 1826), ix.

29 SLC, *Report*.

30 See, e.g., the opinion of Lord Deas in *Thomson v. James* (1855) 18 D. 1, 26–27.

31 Hector L. MacQueen, *MacQueen and Thomson on Contract Law in Scotland* (6th edn) (Bloomsbury Professional, 2024), para.2.41–2.43.

32 John Paul Sheridan, *Contract Law in Flux*, [2018] JLSS, accessible at https://www.lawscot.org.uk/members/journal/issues/vol-63-issue-01/contract-law-in-flux/.

33 See Bogle, *Contract Before the Enlightenment*, 71.

34 Consider that the majority of Scots textbooks on the subject of the law pertaining to voluntary obligations are in fact styled as texts on 'contract' or 'contract law': e.g., *MacQueen and Thomson*; *Woolman and Black on Contract* (W. Green, 2018); William W. McBryde, *Contract Law in Scotland* (3rd edn) (W. Green, 2007), among others. Even in more advanced monographs, modern authors appear to prefer to speak of a 'generalised idea of contract' – seemingly subsuming the idea of unilateral promise under this heading – than of the generalised idea of 'obligations' and 'voluntary obligations' in fact presented in Stair's work: See Stephen Bogle, *Contract Before the Enlightenment: The Ideas of James Dalrymple, Viscount Stair, 1619–1695* (Oxford University Press, 2023), 1.

35 See Martin Hogg, *Obligations* (2nd edn) (Avizandum, 2006), paras.1.03–1.04; David M. Walker, *The Law of Contracts and Related Obligations in Scotland* (3rd edn) (T&T Clark, 1995), para.1.3. Insofar as it makes sense to speak of Scots 'contract theory', it can be said that the 'mix' to be found in the 'mixed legal system' of Scotland is 'not simply that of the traditional mix of Roman with Common law that one would expect from a so-called 'mixed legal system', but also a mix of natural law, Aristotelian ideas, with a conception of law as a rational discipline emphasising the human will as a constituting obligational force [...] the peculiar obligational framework of Scots law gives its contract law distinctive characteristics, both conceptual and functional, from that of the Common law': Hogg, *Perspectives*, 643.

36 SLC, *Report*.

37 See G. Campbell H. Paton, 'Comparison Between the Institutions and Other Institutional Writings' in Walker (ed.), *Stair Tercentenary Studies*, 201. To write an *Institute* or *Institution*, is definitionally to write a work of instruction. With that said, it is certainly possible – indeed, perhaps even likely – that 'Stair may have had in mind not only instruction, but also the protection of Scots law within the Cromwellian Union between England and Scotland, when he wrote his Institutions in the 1660s': Rahmatian, *Institutional Writers*, 45, citing Gordon M. Hutton, 'Purposes and Pattern of the Institutions: Stair's Aim in Writing the Institutions' in Walker (ed.), *Stair Tercentenary Studies*, 82 and John Cairns, 'Institutional Writings in Scotland Reconsidered' in Albert Kiralfy and Hector L. MacQueen (eds), *New Perspectives in Scottish Legal History* (Frank Cass, 1984), 90.

38 Ibid., para.1.12.

39 See (among other things, the literature on this point is vast) Stephen Thomson, *Mixed Jurisdiction and the Scottish Legal Tradition: Reconsidering the Concept of Mixture*, [2014] J. Civ. L. Stud. 7.

40 'Legal education in Scotland was [in the Eighteenth Century into the middle of the Twentieth] in its general pattern much like continental legal education. And the views of the professors had a weight which was like that of the continental professors [though this authority did wane from the mid-Nineteenth into the Twentieth Century]. The "institutional writers" were not a tartan-and-heather phenomenon, but a natural part of the system': George L. Gretton, *Legal Science or Law Lite?* [2006] JLSS 44, 44.

41 John W.G. Blackie and Niall R. Whitty, 'Scotland and the New *Ius Commune*' in Hector L. MacQueen (ed.), *Scots Law into the 21st Century: Essays in Honour of W. A. Wilson* (W. Green, 1996), 79–81.

42 Rahmatian, *Institutional Writers*, 43.

43 The phenomenon is not limited to Scotland: Professor Michelon's recent observation that 'never has so much been written about the law by so many' was posited, rightly, without jurisdictional limitation. See Claudio Michelon, *The Authority of Doctrinal Scholarship*, [2024] Edinburgh Private Law Blog, accessible at https://blogs.ed.ac.uk/private-law/2024/10/11/the-authority-of-doctrinal-scholarship/. For Scotland specifically, see Kenneth G.C. Reid, 'The Third Branch of the Profession: The Rise of the Academic Lawyer in Scotland' in MacQueen (ed.), *Scots Law into the 21st Century*.

44 Of which, see Reid, 'The Third Branch of the Profession', at 40.

45 Of which, see https://edinburghlawseminars.co.uk/book-series.

46 Niall R. Whitty, *Unjustified Enrichment in Scots Law: Time for Consolidation, not Reappraisal?* [2022] Edinburgh Private Law Blog, accessible at https://blogs.ed.ac.uk/private

-law/2022/05/05/unjustified-enrichment-in-scots-law-time-for-consolidation-not-reappraisal/.

47 Martin Hogg, 'Codification of Private Law: Scots Law at the Crossroads of Common and Civil Law' in Kit Barker, Karen Fairweather and Ross Grantham (eds), *Private Law in the 21st Century* (Hart, 2017), 107, at 113.

48 Michelon, *The Authority of Doctrinal Scholarship.*

49 Rahmatian, *Institutional Writers*, 45 (citing Ford: 'it was Stair, more than any other jurist writing in Scotland during the Seventeenth Century, who had tried to promote the idea that all laws must be derived from the exercise of sovereignty by a lawgiver' – John Ford, *Law and Opinion in Scotland During the Seventeenth Century* (Hart, 2007), at 572).

50 Stair, *Institutions*, I, 1, 15.

51 D. Neil MacCormick, *Legal Reasoning and Legal Theory* (Clarendon, 1978), 58. It is no exaggeration to say that Stair's understanding, as expressed here, is even less fashionable in 2025 than it was at MacCormick's time of writing in 1978.

52 Or, for that matter, even democrats: See D. Neil MacCormick, *The Democratic Intellect and the Law*, [1985] Legal Studies 172, 182.

53 'By virtue of this Treaty [...] no Alteration [is to] be made in Laws which concern private Right, except for evident Utility of the Subjects within Scotland': Treaty of Union (1707), Article XVIII.

54 Ford, *Law and Opinion*, 571.

55 *In rebus novis constituendis evidens esse utilitas debet, ut recedatur ab eo iure, quod diu aequum visum est:* Dig.1.4.2 (Ulpian).

56 Birks, 'Definition and Division', 28.

57 Contract (Formation) (Scotland) Bill Informal Consultation on Working Draft – 1 September to 3 November 2017, para.1.11.

58 See Bell, *Commentaries*, 293–294.

59 Cicero, *De Officiis*, 1.33.

60 Law Commissions Act 1965, s.3 (1).

61 Lord Hunter, *Law Reform: The Scottish Law Commission*, [1988] Jur. Rev. 158, 163.

62 Alan Watson, *Slave Law in the Americas* (The University of Georgia Press, 1989), xii.

63 Alan Watson, *Failures of the Legal Imagination* (University of Pennsylvania Press, 1988).

64 Alan Watson, *Society and Legal Change* (2nd edn) (Temple University Press, 2001).

65 Ibid., xviii.

66 Hector L. MacQueen, *Invincible or Just a Flesh-Wound: The Holy Grail of Scots Law* (2014) Legal Information Management 2, 10.

Chapter 1

VISCOUNT STAIR AND THE TAXONOMY OF PRIVATE LAW 'OBLIGATIONS'

Introduction

In the words of Professor Gordley, '[b]efore the Nineteenth century, the English had a learned [legal] tradition, but not an intellectual tradition'.[1] It was not until 1790 that a Common lawyer – John Joseph Powell[2] – ventured to write 'an essay upon the law of contracts and agreements'.[3] Prior to this, 'there was scarcely any Common law literature on contracts beyond a few pages in Blackstone and the reports of decided cases'.[4] There was no meaningful organisation of the relevant material and absolutely no systemic taxonomical or even doctrinally rational structure for the law in this area.[5] Thus, it can be justly said that it was not until the turn of the nineteenth century that English lawyers came to 'arrive at the point that the Romans had reached centuries before and that they did so only by borrowing from Civil law'.[6] This process of borrowing was one which the borrowers were philosophically underequipped for; 'the philosophy [of the Civilian and natural lawyers] was almost unintelligible to [these] Nineteenth Century jurists. Consequently, the treatise writers often borrowed superficially, repeating the phrases of the natural lawyers with little understanding of their original meaning. They often borrowed selectively, neglecting doctrines that seemed alien and repugnant.'[7]

The position of 'Scots contract law' could not be more different.[8] The idea of 'contract' as a legal category within an ordered taxonomical structure 'had existed in ancient Rome and in much of Continental Europe from medieval times and had flourished as law even in poor, remote Scotland from the Seventeenth Century'.[9] Instrumental to the development of an ordered idea of 'contract law' was Viscount Stair,[10] whose opus *Institutions of the Law of Scotland* was first published in 1681,[11] though it had circulated in manuscript form for some decades before this.[12] As was indicated in the introduction, however, Stair did not conceptualise an autonomous 'law of contract'. While any scholar who wishes to understand the theory of Scots contract law must indeed start with Stair,[13] such scholars must also appreciate the fact that for Stair 'contract law' is not an independent, primary topic sequestered to its own corner of the legal system, but in fact a mere part of a broader descriptive taxonomical class.[14] That taxonomical class is the 'law of obligations', which is itself divided into two orders, 'voluntary' and 'involuntary' obligations.[15] The order 'voluntary obligations' further subdivides into two families: 'promise' and 'contract',[16] with the word 'paction' sometimes being used by Stair as a synonym of 'contract'.[17]

This chapter seeks to explore the ordered taxonomy of 'obligations' developed by Stair in his *Institutions* to demonstrate that – notwithstanding apparent convergence between Scots and English law in respect of 'contracts' – the Scottish 'law of contract' is, conceptually, a different beast from the equivalent topic in Common, and indeed Civilian, legal jurisdictions. Stair's intellectual framework takes account of how all 'obligations' are formed, wherever such obligations stand in the taxonomical hierarchy: this provides a model of conceptual unity which the SLC's proposed Contract Formation Bill threatens to destroy. Within Stair's schema, there is no place for anything like the 'contract-tort' fallacy and so there is scope for scholars and jurisprudents to understand the operation of 'personal rights' without (overly) caring about the provenance of such rights. More than this, since Stair proved himself not only willing, but eminently able to deviate from the strictures of Roman jurisprudence and thought where such was intellectually expedient, it might be said that Stair has provided Scotland with an essentially unique legal system which can stand as an interesting point of comparison for those standing in purely Common or Civilian legal systems. Indeed, it appears that Stair's innovations in conceptualising a bipartite division of 'obligations' were so fundamentally un-Roman that his juristic successors – even those with a keen interest in taxonomy and organisation – as yet find it difficult to grasp. Nonetheless, this chapter seeks to make the case that the schema remains, essentially, worthy of comparative study and – more than this – that its abrogation by legislative fiat would be, plainly, tragic.

Since learned lawyers have, generally, been taught[18] – as those schooled in the Civilian tradition tend to be[19] – that obligations are 'principally split into a division of two species',[20] Stair's bipartite division might, then, seem instinctively intuitive. In fact, this is not the case as the basic Roman division of obligations was not between 'voluntary' and 'involuntary' obligations, but rather between those arising from contract and those arising from delict.[21] Gaius, of course, rather overstated the matter (though he cast a long shadow) in identifying this bifurcation and it was for Tribonian to expand the bipartite divide into a quadripartite one,[22] introducing what Birks termed the 'hopeless quasi-categories'[23] (i.e. obligations arising *quasi ex contractu* and *quasi ex maleficio*

– 'as though from contract' and 'as though from wrongdoing' respectively).[24] In popular (insofar as such a term can be used where lawyers are concerned) legal imagination, however, contract and delict, or to adopt the Anglo-American formulation contract and tort, remain seen as the 'fundamental sources of obligations'[25] with quasi-contract standing as a 'less defined "third pillar"'[26] and quasi-delict largely forgotten outwith (and to an extent perhaps even within) Scotland.[27]

The genius of Stair's categorisation of obligations was to reduce the number of prospective causes of obligations from four to two once again, though in doing so also to recognise that 'agreement' and 'wrongdoing' do not reign supreme as principal causes of *obligationes*. 'Contracts', for Stair, may have had a 'common consensual basis', but for him it was *voluntas* – will – rather than singular 'consent' that generated legal bonds where such were not otherwise imposed by law. It is thus an inescapable fact that Stair's schema is non-Roman, though lawyers from furth of the jurisdiction have nonetheless been tempted to parse his taxonomy in terms familiar to the Civil (and increasingly the Common) law.[28] Birks, for instance, considered Stair's schema as ultimately involving 'obligations arising by agreement and obligations imposed without regard to agreement'.[29] This gloss manifestly assigns 'contract' a principal place in the schema even while recognising the broader importance of his organisation of 'obligations' as a unitary category, given the focus on 'agreement' as opposed to (what was in fact for Stair principal) 'will' or *voluntas*. In doing this, Birks was not, alas, behaving in an egregious manner that no Scots-educated scholar would do; in fact, a great deal of Scots legal commentary, written at all levels, reduces the substantive law of 'voluntary obligations' to the shorthand title 'contract'.

It is here submitted that the relative inconsequence of 'contract' and 'delict' as categories for Stair has proven difficult for many commentators to grapple with.[30] Yet it is nonetheless plain that 'agreement' does not play the definitive role in respect of obligations-formation in the Scottish legal system that it does in other systems, of whatever 'legal family'. At the core of Stair's division of obligations into those arising from human will and those which are 'obediential' (and so ultimately imposed by law) is the recognition that it is 'engagement' that is indicative of the exercise of will required to bring an *ex voluntate* obligation into being. Consequently, this chapter seeks to elucidate, in modern and accessible terms, the intellectual framework concerned with the formation of 'voluntary obligations' elucidated by Stair in his *Institutions*. In doing so, it seeks to make the case that the conceptual unity that Stair's schema provides is, unequivocally, a good thing and that fragmentation of what is presently a unitary topic of law would have a deleterious impact on legal rationality and so the interests of justice.

‘Promises’ and ‘Contracts’

Promises and contracts are distinct from one another in Stair’s view – as expressly followed in Scots case law[31] – because the former is ‘that which is simple and pure, and hath not implyed [*sic*] as a condition in its being the acceptance of another’, while the latter requires an acceptance of an offer to become obligatory.[32] They are also distinct from one another by dint of the fact that contracts are unique among ‘obligations’,[33] in that they are reciprocal – that is, necessarily possessed of ‘mutuality’.[34] That is to say, while ordinarily in cases involving ‘obligations’ – in the Roman sense of that term – one party stands as ‘debtor’ bound to perform some action for, or render payment to, the other who stands as ‘creditor’,[35] in the case of ‘contracts’ – being that such are bilaterally constituted (i.e. creatures of consent and consensus)[36] both or all parties must necessarily stand simultaneously as creditor *and* debtor *vis-à-vis* one another.[37] In other words, while in a promissory or indeed delictual obligation, liability is essentially unidirectional, with the debtor finding themselves liable to perform something for another because of the commission of a single juridical act,[38] with no reciprocity on the part of the creditor, a contract is ‘a deed of two, the offeror and the acceptor’.[39] Two juridical acts must occur for the contract to be brought into being; hence, both parties are bound to perform something for the other, even if that performance is – as in the case of a gratuitous contract[40] – limited to one party’s simple receipt of the performance to be rendered by the other.[41]

In the words of Lord Drummond Young, ‘mutuality is a fundamental aspect of the Scots law of contract. Indeed, it can be regarded as an essential feature of Scottish bilateral and multilateral contracts in broadly the same way as consideration is an essential feature of English contracts (although the two clearly fulfil different functions).’[42] Promises, by contrast, are not mutual; they are invariably unilaterally constituted and binding only on the promisor. They may be conditional, not in the sense that they require an acceptance (for, as shall be discussed, an act of the will which requires acceptance to be effectual is not a ‘promise’, but is merely an ‘offer’ which requires ‘acceptance’ for the creation of an effectual obligation),[43] but rather in the sense that a suspensive condition (e.g. the birth of a child; a person’s attainment of a certain age; the discovery of a missing pet)[44] may need to be purified in order for the obligation to be enforceable.[45] While the need for performance of a contract may likewise be suspended until the purification of a condition,[46] for that contract to have come into being in the first place the parties to it will need to have come together in agreement – demonstrating *consensus in idem*, meaning here that the offeror can be taken to have objectively known what has been offered and the offeree can be taken to have objectively understood what they have accepted – which is necessarily a bipartite process.[47]

The complex terminology which has come to be used in this section of the article throws into focus a significant semantic problem that plagues philosophical analyses in respect of obligations law: the plethora of overlapping terminology and inescapable imprecision of the English language.[48] There is, in jurisprudence, a need to distinguish – or indeed to compare – legal concepts such as 'obligation', 'promise' and 'contract' – to say nothing of 'mutuality', 'unilaterality/bilaterality', 'gratuitousness/onerousness' and so on, but these terms do not have static, fixed meanings across time, space or jurisdiction. Within modern Scots law, there is – if not a crisis – certainly a deep-rooted, long-standing problem pertaining to the 'fundamental structural language' used within the legal system.[49] This is in part[50] because the jurisdiction has on the one hand an intellectual inheritance which includes a reasoned taxonomic framework and structure for the law of obligations,[51] but also has on the other a deep political connection to a nation with a distinct legal tradition which does not much care for systematisation, rationalisation or taxonomical order in law.[52]

Sharing a common vernacular and apex civil court – but crucially not legal language – with this neighbouring nation means, inevitably, that the fundamental structural language of the Scottish system will be subjected to what Berman describes as 'deforming tendencies'[53] – albeit that the deformation arises through use over time as well as arising from a process of 'like-for-like' translation, as Berman envisaged in his work.[54] The problem of deformation of the legal system's fundamental structural language is compounded by the very fact that language is often used loosely or imprecisely even by learned writers attempting to identify taxonomic order within the legal system[55] – as, indeed, Stair's writing itself so often exemplifies.[56] Indeed, considering Stair's use of the term 'promise', it is readily apparent that 'promise' – as 'act of engagement' used to create a binding obligation – is not sufficiently separated from 'Promise' as descriptive shorthand term denoting 'enforceable unilaterally constituted obligation' in the *Institutions.* Consequently, the separation between the differing conceptual uses of this term is not meaningfully demarcated in either historical or modern sources or case law. This can – and does – make meaningful comparative scholarship challenging and might go some way to explaining why 'Promise' can be justifiably described as 'the neglected obligation in European Private Law'.[57]

There is consequently a need for Scots jurisprudents – and teachers of law must lead the charge, of course, being that they are at the front-line of instructing future academics, practitioners and judges – to take greater care in their use of language in writing and instruction. Clarity of language is necessary for clarity of thought and clarity of thought is a prerequisite of reasoned jurisprudence. Consequently, to meet the principal objectives of this book, the essential meaning of certain key terms used in the English language in connection with the law of obligations must be clarified; as it stands, many key terms used by Scots scholars, judges and jurisprudents would not be properly understood by English-language speakers trained in most other jurisdictions. Fortunately, most of the 'heavy lifting' has already been done by Hogg,[58] however his is not the last word on the topic and much of what he discusses bears repeating, and further critical examination, here.

'Obligations' and 'Fundamental Structural Language'

I have elsewhere described Professor Hogg's *Obligations: Law and Language* as 'magisterial'.[59] I stand by this assessment here. This great work provides a justification for the search for 'default' or 'core' meanings of so-called 'fundamental structural language'. 'Fundamental structural language' can be defined as 'the lexicon comprised of those basic terms which are used by "external observers" of obligational relationships – most often being lawyers, legislators and jurists – to "make sense" of the law of obligations conceptually, as well as of specific undertakings in particular'.[60] The justification for determining an accurate lexicon of 'fundamental structural language' is obvious; 'without shared, default understandings of the fundamental structural language of the law of obligations, any attempt to create taxonomies of obligations would be impossible: if judge A understood the nature of obligations described as "mutual" to mean one thing, judge B understood them to mean another, and judge C to mean something else, the point in employing such a fundamental description would be entirely destroyed'.[61]

Firstly, the terms 'unilaterality' and 'bilaterality' must be clarified, particularly as Common lawyers – and so most legally literate speakers of English – are used to speaking of 'unilateral contracts', a term which – properly applying Scots fundamental structural language – is oxymoronic.[62] The term 'unilateral' itself appears to be – in legal use, at least – a product of Scots as 'in the period before 1830, almost all uses of "unilateral" are in Scottish legal works'.[63] Indeed, 'the English words "unilateral" and "bilateral" do not appear in the English lexicon until the late Eighteenth Century'.[64] Though the terms – and variations, such as 'monolateral'[65] – were used in Scots pleadings, Stair himself did not employ either of the terms 'unilateral' or 'bilateral'.[66] Ironically, the first use of the term appears to have been in describing a contract of caution as 'unilateral',[67] providing precedent – if not justification – for the later Common law usage. Despite this early use, by the time of George Joseph Bell – widely regarded as Scotland's last 'Institutional writer'[68] (though he in fact wrote a *Commentary*, and a book of *Principles*, rather than an *Institution* or *Institute* as his juristic forebearers had done)[69] – 'we see a clear alignment of usage of the terminology of "unilateral/bilateral" towards "sense one" [of Hogg's own descriptive account of the terms]'.[70] That is to say, in Scotland 'unilateral' denotes 'an obligational relationship whose constitution involves one party only', while 'bilateral' denotes 'an obligational relationship whose constitution involves two parties'.[71] Naturally, 'the variation "multilateral" denot[es] an obligation whose constitution involves three or more parties'.[72]

The terminology of 'unilateral contract' thus ought to be rejected in Scots law. Contracts, necessarily, involve two or more parties coming together and engaging with one another so as to bring into being an obligation by force of their will and consensus. This obligation is necessarily bi- or multilateral, based on the above definitions, and likewise it is necessarily mutual, in the sense that each of the parties who created the obligation are bound to perform something for the other(s), even if such is simply permitting or allowing the performance of the other(s).[73] 'Mutuality', in this sense, maps on to the Greek term *διπλευρος* employed by Stair, though not perfectly, and so its counterpart and jural opposite can be identified as *μονόπλευρος*. In this sense, then, all 'contracts' are *διπλευρος*, or 'mutual', since the parties are correlatively bound to perform acts for one another (even if the action in question amounts to nothing more than receiving a benefit), while all other obligations (save *negotiorum gestio*, which like contract gives rise to a two-sided action)[74] – being *vincula iuris* bonding debtor-to-creditor – are *μονόπλευρος*, one-sided, as only one party can be compelled to perform under the obligation.[75]

One-sidedness should not be equated with the notion of 'gratuitousness', however, as the English term 'gratuitous' too is a part of the fundamental structural language of the Scots law of obligations and is distinguishable from the concept denoted by the Greek *μονόπλευρος*. As Hogg has observed, 'the three specifically legal usages of the term "gratuitous" given in the OED derive from Scottish rather than English legal sources';[76] hence it is unsurprising that 'it is in Scotland that we find the structural, contrasting language of gratuitous and onerous most clearly established'[77] – albeit that this taxonomical divide was received from Canonist thought[78] and 'the history of the Scottish use of the terms "gratuitous" and "onerous" is a troubled one'.[79]

Although Scots law does not and has never recognised the Common law concept of 'consideration' as necessary for the formation of contracts, or any other obligations, the term 'gratuitous' in modern Scots usage has seemingly come to mean 'an obligation or other juridical act undertaken for no consideration'.[80] In Stair's usage, it appears to have mapped on to his idea of *μονόπλευρος*, but since at least the time of Lord Bankton's *Institute* the term has been employed to emphasise that while 'generally a recompense, promise of covenant for a reward is required by the law of England; in as much as a nude contract or naked promise is not binding for want of *quid pro quo*, or good consideration [...] in our law, such promises would be intended or understood gratuitous, and the party is bound to perform them'.[81] In other words, 'gratuitous' can in Scots law be interpreted as meaning 'given without consideration [in the English sense of that term]', with 'onerous' correspondingly understood as 'given with consideration', notwithstanding the fact that 'consideration' is not generally a feature of the Scots law of obligations.

This is not altogether a particularly meaningful use of the terms 'gratuitous' and 'onerous'. It may be helpful for scholars and teachers to employ the terms in the sense used above, as such serves as a useful means of clearly and simply distinguishing Scots from English law, but ultimately using the terms in this way does nothing to clarify the practical meaning of the words within the Scots legal system itself. Indeed, the ongoing 'definitional imprecision has continued down to the modern age, with attempts to locate a single meaning for the terms resulting in disagreement among academic commentators'.[82] This dispute, concerned with the meaning of the terms 'gratuitous' and 'onerous', is not bereft of practical consequences, given the language used within the Requirements of Writing (Scotland) Act 1995, which in s.1 provides the general rule that 'writing shall not be required for the constitution of a contract, unilateral obligation or trust', before going on to provide that, exceptionally, 'a written document [...] shall be required for [...] a gratuitous unilateral obligation except an obligation undertaken in the course of business'. Since the passing of this legislation, clarifying the definition of 'gratuitous' has taken on a renewed practical importance, yet in the nigh 30 years since the passing of the 1995 Act no definitive consensus – or even definitive *lex*[83] from the Scottish courts – has been achieved.

At the risk of adding simply one more commentator's voice to the expanding and expansive pile, it is here submitted that within Scots law the term 'gratuitous' should be taken to denote those circumstances in which 'A, who is to tender some value to B, lacks any expectation [if not any hope] of a payment/performance from B'.[84] Correspondingly, 'onerous' can be consequently defined as 'where A, who is to tender some value to B [...] expects a payment/performance from B'.[85] On this reading, then, 'gratuitous' obligations are those which – adapting the words of Thomson – involve 'giving or doing something for nothing'.[86] 'Onerous' obligations, by contrast, are those which are undertaken in the expectation of gain. If, on winning the lottery, I promise, or agree,[87] to pay my brother £100,000 out of a sense of fraternal piety, the obligation I undertake can be described as gratuitous as I have no expectation that I will benefit from the transaction.[88] By contrast, if I promise or agree to pay him that same sum should he find and return my lost dog to me, that transaction is onerous; I am bound to render performance, but only in the event that my expectation of personal benefit is realised (the promise is issued *sub conditione* and while there is no duty on the part of my brother to find my dog. It merely means that if he does so, I am bound to pay him the stipulated sum).[89]

The utility of adopting the terminology of *μονόπλευρος*, *διπλευρος* (and perhaps *πολυπλευρος* in cases of multilateral obligations) is consequently apparent, as these concepts provide meaningful juridical signifiers to the directionality of obligations in a way that, unfortunately, the distinct ideas of 'gratuitousness' and 'onerousness' have been taken to do by some.[90] Taking the discussion of 'fundamental structural language' conducted above into account, an obligation created by way of promise can be described as necessarily unilateral, as it is created by a single juridical act, and necessarily *μονόπλευρος*, because only the promisor is bound to perform, but a promise may be described as either gratuitous or onerous depending on the promisor's purpose in constituting it.[91] By contrast, a contractual obligation is necessarily bi- or multilateral, since the constitution of a contract requires agreement (and so at least two juridical acts). Since the obligation which arises *ex contractu* binds both (or all, if the contract is multilateral) of the parties to it, both (or all) parties are required to perform something by dint of the obligation. Contracts, then, are necessarily *διπλευρος* (or *πολυπλευρος* if multilaterally constituted), although here the English-language term 'mutual' can be preferred to the Greek (although to do so would, it is thought, cause issues given the complexity of 'mutuality' as a concept within Scots law). Just as in the case of obligations created by promise, contracts may be either gratuitous or onerous, depending on the overarching nature of the agreement; if the parties are agreed that one party should perform something for nothing, that is gratuitous, while if there is some *quid pro quo* then the contract can meaningfully be called 'onerous'.

With these concepts clarified, it should at this juncture be stressed that the terms 'promise' and 'contract' are, themselves, part of the 'fundamental structural language' of Scots obligations law. Consequently, although it is important to emphasise – as has been done here – that 'promise' and 'contract' can evidently be distinguished from one another, one cannot lose sight of the fact that the concepts do share some core common features. Being that they are each a part of the same taxonomical order, it should be stressed that both unilateral obligatory promises and bilateral obligatory contracts principally arise from acts of human will.[92] They are created, therefore, by 'acts of will', as identified and discussed by Stair. Naturally, not any act of will suffices to create a binding obligation; accordingly, Stair 'distinguish[es] three acts in the will, Desire, Resolution and Ingagement [i.e., engagement]',[93] with only the last of these resulting in 'a diminution of freedom, and constituting of power in another, whereby he may restrain, or constrain to the doing or performing of that whereof we have given him power of exaction'.[94] Given that it can be said with some certainty that 'Stair's pronouncement [on the theory of voluntary obligations] was sufficiently authoritative to be followed by others and to represent the modern law',[95] further examination of his tripartite distinction of 'acts of the will' is warranted.[96]

'Acts of the Will': 'Desire', 'Resolution' and 'Engagement'

'Desire', for Stair, is defined as 'a tendency or inclination of the will towards its object, and it is the first motion thereof, which is not sufficient to constitute a right'.[97] In other words, 'desire' maps onto an uncommunicated idea that one might like to create and be bound by an obligation, for whatever reason. Being an internal mental event, it does not result in the creation of any binding promise or paction and does not allow anyone to take legal action against the desirer (such, indeed, is little more than a statement of the obvious: if the desire is uncommunicated, absent telepathy no one can know of the silent wishes of the desirer). Fundamentally, the idea of 'desire' is simply the pragmatic recognition that any expression of will must be preceded by some process of cerebral reasoning, which presupposes that the juridical actor has sufficient 'capacity', in law, to undertake juridically effective acts.[98]

The next 'act of the will' – 'resolution' – does not itself[99] suffice to create any obligation (whether promissory or contractual) either.[100] This concept is defined as 'a determinate purpose to do that which is desired' and, like 'desire', does not serve to create any obligation 'because, whatsoever is resolved or purposed, may be without fault altered'.[101] Examples of 'resolution' abound in Common law (by which is meant Anglo-American) case law,[102] although more often than not the concept goes by the moniker of 'invitation to treat'.[103] Essentially, 'resolution' can be understood as some action or expression which indicates to the world at large, or indeed to a particular person, that a prospective debtor is interested in potentially entering into a binding obligation. Necessarily, 'resolution' falls short of an absolute commitment to enter into a transaction, however, and it does not 'conferreth or stateth a power of exaction in another'.[104] For an obligation to be created, the prospective obligant must demonstrate 'engagement' – though this 'engagement' may be with a particular named person,[105] or with the world at large,[106] provided that an identifiable subject may lay claim to the right to act as creditor *viz* the debtor's obligation.[107]

'As freedom began, where obedience ended; so [e]ngagement begins where freedom ends; it being our voluntar oblieging of ourselves, where by nature we are free; every such obligation, is a diminution of that freedom, for thereby, we are [...] constrained to some performances contrair to our natural liberty'.[108] Essentially, in Stair's view, though all persons are axiomatically bound by *ex lege*, or 'obediential' obligations (for instance, to provide aliment for one's children,[109] to afford reparation for damage done and affronts to liberty, *inter alia*,[110] or to afford restitution in cases of unjustified enrichment,[111] or *negotiorum gestio*[112] etc.), they are otherwise free to act as they please, as and until they bind themselves to perform something for another by engagement. When they have committed some act of engagement – that is, when they have exercised their will in order make clear their intention to do something which another can enforce – they become bound to perform their undertaking and lose their freedom to abstain from such performance.[113] Hence, in Stair's philosophy – as in positive Scots law, says he,[114] following *Sharp v. Sharp*[115] – 'every paction produceth action, *omne verbum de ore fideli cadit in debitum* [and every word spoken in faith creates a debt]'.[116]

'Engagement': Promise, Offer and Acceptance

It is obvious that the concept of 'engagement' is core to Stair's concept of 'voluntary obligations'. 'Engagement' can thus be understood to amount to any overt act or expression of the will of the engager which commits that engager to some legal consequence (or, in other words, the law can be said to 'respond to' engagement). Quite what that legal consequence is will depend on the circumstances of the engagement: if the engagement is not conditional on acceptance, then the engagement itself serves to create a binding obligation tying the engager, as debtor, to the beneficiary of the undertaking, who stands as creditor. This obligation can be identified as 'promise', strictly so-called. 'Bearing in mind the stringent consequences of a valid promise [...] [then-Lord President Gill] consider[ed] that a promise is binding only if the promisor's own words are clear and unambiguous' in the 2013 case of *Regus Maxim Ltd. v. Bank of Scotland*,[117] a position which would appear to be consistent with Stair's view that 'word[s] spoken in faith' – not merely actions – create debts.[118] Although the position of Scots law was changed quite radically with the introduction of the Contract (Rights of Third Parties) (Scotland) Act 2017,[119] for Stair engagement between two or more persons could also create a *jus quaesitum tertio*,[120] binding the engagers from the moment of engagement to honour the agreed 'article in favour of a third party'.[121] There is no need for communication of the engagement to the beneficiary of a promise or *jus quaesitum tertio* – the beneficiary need not accept the benefit of the obligation, nor need they know of the obligation's existence nor need they even exist as a 'person' at the time of the obligation's creation – for the party or parties who engaged to create it to be bound by its terms. The expression of the relevant article as agreed between the parties themselves, alone, was sufficient at Common law. This analysis of the operation and effect of 'engagement', naturally, has consequences for the rules concerned with the formation of 'contracts' also.

A 'contract', unlike a 'promise' or Common law *jus quaesitum tertio*, can only come into being if the creditor and debtor in the obligation (bearing in mind that as contracts are necessarily *διπλευρος* – two-sided, or mutual/reciprocal) each agree to be bound by the terms of the obligation. Essentially, the engagement of one is insufficient to bind both; there must be reciprocal acts of engagement demonstrating that the parties have achieved *consensus in idem*.[122] This process of reciprocal engagement can be described and analysed in terms of 'offer' + 'acceptance' = 'contract'; however, this analysis does not map on perfectly, or even neatly, to the 'functionally equivalent'[123] process for contract-creation in Anglo-American law, since that process is typically conceived of as an 'exchange of promises'[124] – a view most unhelpful in Stair's schema[125] – and the general rule therein is that 'an acceptance has no legal effect until it is communicated to the offeror'.[126] As Bogle notes, however, 'if [Stair's] approach to acceptance is compared to his treatment of promises and third-party rights then, theoretically, the offeror does not need to know of the acceptance in order for an obligation to exist. It is the moment of acceptance when the formation of the obligation is completed, not necessarily receipt of acceptance.'[127] Bogle's observation correlates with McBryde's opinion of the position in modern Scots 'contract law': 'instead of saying that acceptance must be communicated, it may be more accurate to state that the offeree must go beyond the deliberative stage [i.e., the stage of "resolution"]. What is required is (1) intention to accept, followed by (2) actions showing the intention to be irrevocable.'[128]

In Stair's scheme, then, it can be said that the concepts 'promise', 'offer' and 'acceptance' may each be identified as species of engagement, albeit species with different consequences. *Jus quaesitum tertio*, for its part, arises as a consequence of reciprocal acts of engagement (offer and acceptance) and so can be distinguished from 'promise', 'offer' and 'acceptance'; it comes into being as an obligation and, as obligations are capable of being 'reified',[129] can be conceived of as a *res*, or 'thing', from the moment of its creation.[130] In the sense that *jus quaesitum tertio* immediately creates an obligation, it can be likened to a 'promise' where that term is used as a synonym for the obligation created by the unilateral act of 'engagement' known as 'promise', but is distinct and distinguishable from the unilateral act of 'engagement' known as 'promise', which for its part can be compared with 'offer' and 'acceptance' as instruments of demonstrating parties' will. This has significant consequences for any analyses concerned with the creation of voluntary obligations and, indeed, demonstrates the importance of clarity of terminology and the need for jurisprudents to consider the philosophical underpinnings of the theory of voluntary obligation formation as articulated by Stair. In the absence of such, there is the manifest potential for scholars – and so students and thereafter practitioners and judges – to be misled or to mislead themselves.

Such is in fact demonstrated in a discussion of 'a few tricky problems surrounding unilateral promises' considered by Hogg.[131] Here, Hogg notes that 'unilateral promise should by definition never place any duties upon the party to whom the promise has been made'.[132] This is so since a promise is – unlike a contract – necessarily *μονόπλευρος*, although Hogg does not use that term. An analysis that omits consideration of Stair's concept of promise as a mode of engagement which creates a binding obligation as distinct from 'promise' as the term denoting the created, extant, unilateral obligation resulting from that engagement is bound to run into difficulty when faced with the question of what should be taken to occur in those 'situation[s] where a promise chooses to accept the promise'.[133] If 'promise' is conceived only as the species of voluntary obligation created, then acceptance of the promise would seem to throw up a conceptual difficulty; one has to grapple with the idea that the acceptance might have the effect of converting one type of nominate obligation ('promise') into a different species of nominate obligation ('contract').

Conceptualised in such terms, the Stair Memorial Encyclopaedia (in an entry written by Black) turns its face against this notion, stating unequivocally that 'the juristic nature of the obligation and its character as onerous or gratuitous [note that "onerous" and "gratuitous" here map on to the concepts "mutual" and *μονόπλευρος* respectively] is determined once and for all when it first comes into existence: if at that stage the content of the obligation is not the product of the agreement of the parties there is not then, and there will not subsequently be, a contract between them in relation to the promised performance'.[134] This observation was described as 'theoretically impeccable' by McBryde[135] and finds support in positive case law. As Lord Dunedin observed in *Smith v. Oliver*,[136] 'it is quite well settled by a series of cases that a party cannot turn what is, in its nature, a mere promise into a contract, so as to be allowed to prove it by parole, by simply averring that on the faith of the promise certain things were done by him; that is to say, he cannot turn a promise into a contract by *rei interventus*, so to speak'.[137]

With the greatest of respect to both Professor Black and Lord Dunedin, it is here submitted that these learned jurists have in fact misled themselves as to the nature of 'promise', 'acceptance' and 'contract'. The mistake is most understandable, given the issues in the fundamental structural language of Scots law which have pervaded the jurisdiction particularly in the last hundred or so years, but it is nonetheless a basic category error. 'Promise' and 'contract' – used here in the sense denoting unilateral *μονόπλευρος* obligations and bilateral mutual obligations respectively – are not discrete ossified nominate concepts which exist autonomously of one another as several categories. Rather, the words 'promise' and 'contract' are simply descriptive terms which give justificatory reasons for the particular, enforceable, obligations created through acts of engagement. In other words, they denote modes of creating obligations – that is, 'personal rights' – or describe the mode by which certain obligations have come into being; they are not themselves immutable obligations.[138] As McBryde observes, 'there is no rule of law that an obligation once created is immutable. On the contrary, as much of contract law can demonstrate.'[139]

One cannot then lose sight of the fact that 'promise' and 'contract' are essentially just used as descriptive shorthand terms, not fundamental or basic legal categories. The phraseology of 'unilateral *μονόπλευρος* obligations' and 'bilateral mutual obligations' is consequently preferable for purposes of philosophical and linguistic clarity, but of course such language is unduly cumbersome. Hence, discussion of 'promise' and 'contract' as shorthand should not be abandoned, but those who are to bandy about such terms must be conscious of the fact that in using the words they are employing nothing more than shorthand. Recognition of such would, fundamentally, resolve the issues identified by Hogg and McBryde about the ostensible 'problem' of the 'accepted promise'. McBryde takes the view that though 'there are issues yet to be resolved, but it is thought that if a promise is accepted, in some circumstances, a contract may be created'.[140] Since promise, offer and acceptance are each species of engagement, and it is acts of engagement demonstrating the will of prospective obligants that bring into being enforceable voluntary obligations, it should be obvious that McBryde is correct; the 'acceptance' of a 'promise', being a reciprocal act of engagement, should be taken to conclude a contract between the promisor and the acceptor.[141] If, however, the Bill proposed by the SLC were to be enacted, and 'contract formation' sequestrated from the broader law of voluntary obligations, then this sensible interpretation may seem less intuitively obvious.

Presently, a 'promise' – in the sense of the species of engagement – brings into being an obligation, vesting a personal right in the beneficiary of the promise, instantaneously.[142] This is so even if the beneficiary does not know that the promise has been made.[143] On the other hand, an 'offer', naturally, does not create any obligation due to its conditional – that is to be constructed strictly as 'conditional upon acceptance'[144] – nature. Nonetheless, it is not without legal consequence. Being an 'act of engagement', offers necessarily constitute some 'power of exaction' in the offeree – that power, crucially, not being the power to claim a personal right, but instead being the power to accept the offer, so bringing into existence a mutual bilateral obligation (i.e. a contract). This point, it is thought, is crucial for any analysis of the so-called 'postal acceptance rule' in Scots law; though it is the case that an offer can be withdrawn (and so killed) at any time prior to acceptance,[145] for as long as the offer is 'alive' the offeree enjoys possession of a power conferred upon them by the offeror – the power to reciprocally engage with the offeror by way of acceptance.

Since the offeror must know (or constructively be taken to know, given the objective approach to contract formation)[146] that in sending an offer they open up the possibility of being bound to some obligation (indeed, the act of making the offer necessarily indicates their will to be bound by such), the communication of acceptance of said offer to them is logically nugatory. The offer will either expire at a certain nominated time (e.g. 'close of business on Friday') or after the passage of a reasonable amount of time in the circumstances of the case;[147] the offeror is not placed under a perpetual threat of being bound because of an offer made long ago and forgotten about. Having shown their commitment to entering into a binding obligation through engagement – and having not relieved themselves, as they are able to do, by withdrawing the offer – the offeror should not be able to cry foul when they find themselves bound to an obligation because the offeree's engagement was not effectively communicated to them. Indeed, if receipt of communication is thought so important by the offeror, in a particular transaction, then the nature of party autonomy is such that the offeror can candidly stipulate that the obligation will come into being only on receipt of the acceptance,[148] in the same way that any party can stipulate that acceptance must take a particular form despite the provision of the general rule that 'writing shall not be required for the constitution of a contract, unilateral obligation or trust'.[149]

As Lord President Hamilton observed in the 2007 case of *Cawdor v. Cawdor*, 'the presence or absence of communication to the other party may be an adminicle of evidence in the question whether the statement amounts to a promise in law'[150] and this statement can – being that promises and acceptances are each species of effectual engagement – be applied *mutatis mutandis* to 'acceptances' as well as 'promises'. In essence, then, a party who seeks to claim that they did engage with an offer sufficiently to have 'accepted' it may face evidentiary difficulties in satisfying a court, on the balance of probabilities, that they did in fact engage so as to create a contract as they will necessarily be lacking a significant piece of evidence that the engagement in fact took place. The difficulty, though, is purely evidentiary; it is not an issue of substantive law.

'Acceptance' is thus akin to 'promise' in that it is an act of engagement that brings into being an obligation when the engagement occurs. Logically, communication of the acceptance is not a prerequisite for the enforceability of the resultant obligation brought into being by the acceptance; the obligation comes into being by force of the offeree's will as demonstrated through their act of engagement. Analysing the process of obligation-creation in this way (i.e. in the manner described by Stair) clearly explains the operation of the so-called 'postal acceptance rule' – and indeed would appear to imply that on the basis of general principle acts of engagement such as email, text messaging, voicemail, fax, sky-writing[151] – indeed, any overt act signalling the will of the offeree to accept the offer, even if ultimately unseen, or even undelivered – should be taken to conclude contracts at the moment of commitment on the part of the offeree. Such would presently appear to be consistent with the law as it stands and – being based in logic, reason and the schema of Stair – should be taken to reflect the law of Scotland better than the position as articulated in English case law such as *Entores Ltd. v. Miles Far East Corp.*[152]

Conclusion

From the above, it becomes apparent that Stair's view as expressed in his *Institutions* continues to accurately describe the operation of the Scots law of voluntary obligations today,[153] absent (as in the case of third-party rights) those instances in which the legal position has been expressly altered by statute. Indeed, as MacQueen recently observed, it remains the case that 'perhaps the only serious attempt at [...] philosophical justification [of the Scots law of voluntary obligations], is to be found in Stair's *Institutions*'.[154] Being that Stair's analysis accounts for the formation of both unilateral and bilateral obligations,[155] and unilateral obligations are as significant a part of Scots law as are bilateral[156] (albeit that the latter are more commonly litigated, if not constituted, in the experience of legal practitioners), it is manifestly apparent that his method should be preferred to and promoted over the principally Anglo-American 'offer + acceptance' approach to explaining 'contract formation' by Scots pedagogues. By emphasising 'engagement' as core to the formation of binding voluntary obligations in Scots law, it is here submitted that swathes of case law (including case law from furth of Scotland) can be rationalised in principled, accessible terms to the benefit of Scots students, scholars and jurisprudents. Real and hypothetical examples of the descriptive theories espoused by Stair abound;[157] teachers of Scots law would accordingly do well to consider instructing their students with reference to the first principles of voluntary obligation formation found in the *Institutions*.[158] Indeed, particularly given that so-called 'institutional' works are designed with a principally pedagogical purpose in mind,[159] it should consequently come as no surprise that the exposition of legal principle in a work such as Stair's is instructive, valuable and profoundly useful for those privileged to teach the law.[160]

The above analysis, of course, has practical significance beyond mere pedagogy and indeed it may be thought that poor pedagogical practice has led, at times, to profound misunderstandings of Scots law.[161] Taking Stair's philosophy as the starting point, as the Scots law of voluntary obligations continues to do at its core,[162] means that there are considerable theoretical differences between the respective rules concerning contract formation in Scots and English law, which should resultantly have an effect on how one analyses issues pertaining to the so-called 'postal acceptance rule' between the two jurisdictions. This, in turn, suggests that there is scope for divergence between Scots and English jurisprudence where instances of contract formation between geographically distant parties are concerned; indeed, should English law continue to cleave to the idea that the general position is that 'acceptance' of an 'offer' must be communicated to the offeror in order to be effective, such divergence would be – absent reform of the kind envisaged by the SLC – both inevitable and necessary.[163] While there is certainly a case to be made for the convenience of the cross-border assimilation of law, ultimately it remains the case, as Professor Brodie observed, that 'uncritical adherence [to canons of English law and legal thought] is unlikely to be a good thing'.[164] This is particularly so where, as has been demonstrated, the intellectual background and legal framework is so distinct, and has developed so differently, that much of value would be lost if a part of the framework were to be carved out and isolated by legislative fiat.

Bearing this in mind, it is notable that the so-called 'postal acceptance rule' has not in modern times been meaningfully analysed in terms of Stair's theory of formation of voluntary obligations. Generally – though not exclusively[165] – speaking, Scots jurisprudents, and the Scottish courts,[166] have applied a distinctively Common law method of thinking to those litigated instances of contracts concluded by post (i.e. drawing on interpretation of precedent rather than reasoning from principle), in preference to the logical approach which can be deduced from Stair's broader theory.[167] Nonetheless, as a great many of the essential and distinctive features of Scots law – in particular the Scots law of voluntary obligations – directly arise from Stair's *Institutions*, it is thought that an effort should be made to relate the operation of legal rules in practice to Stair's schema since such has the potential to allow for a more logical and principled development of the law than legislative enactment, or for that matter mere analogical reasoning, can provide. Consequently, though the next chapter of this book moves to focus on the rationalisation of the so-called 'postal acceptance rule' within Stair's schema, it is here submitted that scholars and students might find it useful to engage in a similar process of reasoning in respect of other areas of Scots obligations law.

Notes

1 James Gordley, *The Jurists: A Critical History* (Oxford University Press, 2013), 27.

2 Biographical information on Powell appears to be sparse, though he was certainly a Barrister of the Middle Temple and the author of several editions of a *Treatise upon the Law of Mortgages*, first published in 1785.

3 John J. Powell, *An Essay Upon the Law of Contracts and Agreements* (Chamberlaine et al., 1790).

4 James Gordley, *The Philosophical Origins of Modern Contract Doctrine* (Clarendon Press, 1991), 134.

5 Ironically, the Scots jurist Lord Bankton – in seeking to explain the English 'law of contract' – provided English law with a 'structure and language which it did not see itself as possessing', indicating that the English law of that time could be parsed in Civilian terms: see Bankton, *Institute of the Law of Scotland*, Volume 1 (Fleming, 1751), I, 5, 19; Hogg, *Law and Language*, 36.

6 Gordley, *The Jurists*, 22.

7 Gordley, *Philosophical Origins*, 134.

8 Consistent with its history as a principally Civilian jurisdiction, taxonomy has generally been taken more seriously in Scotland than in the Common law world: see Andrew Burrows, *Understanding the Law of Obligations: Essays on Contract, Tort and Restitution* (Hart Publishing, 1998), 2.

9 Watson, *Slave Law*, at 6–7. Note that 'the notion of a contract as constituted by an obligationary agreement finds expression in *Regiam Majestatem* in the definition of a pact as constituted by "the consent or agreement of two or more persons to the same effect, such as the giving or receiving of something"'. Lubbe, 'Formation of Contract', at 2.

10 See Bogle, *Contract, passim.*

11 (Printed by the Heirs of Andrew Anderson, 1681).

12 Adelyn L.M. Wilson, *The Sources and Method of the Institutions of the Law of Scotland by Sir James Dalrymple, 1st Viscount Stair, with Specific Reference to the Law of Obligations*, [2011] PhD Thesis, University of Edinburgh, at 15. *Per* Ford, the first edition of Stair's *Institutions* was revised and completed in 1662 (Ford, *Law and Opinion*, 72).

13 Hogg, *Perspectives*, 648.

14 Indeed, the term 'obligation' appeared 'in the Roman sense of a *juris vinculum* binding two persons' within *Regiam Majestatem*: Lubbe, 'Formation of Contract', at 6.

15 Stair, *Institutions*, I, 3, 2. Arguably, the duties arising in cases such as *Hedley Byre & Co. Ltd. v. Heller and Partners* [1964] AC 465 – unquestionably tortious in the Common law – may in Scotland be better analysed as generating *ex voluntate* obligations: Brian Pillans, 'Delictual Liability at Common Law' in Joe Thomson (ed.), *Delict* (W. Green, 2007), at 5.12 (fn.5). It should also be noted that 'a sharp divide between contractual and delictual damages was not a feature of [Stair's] thought' (Vernon V. Palmer,

'Contracts of Intellectual Gratification – a Louisiana-Scotland Creation' in Vernon V. Palmer and Elspeth C. Reid, *Mixed Jurisdictions Compared: Private Law in Louisiana and Scotland* (Edinburgh University Press, 2009), 217). The taxonomy presented by Stair is a rationalised structure which seeks to explain what sort of conduct might generate 'obligations', or 'personal rights'; Stair is not describing self-contained topics and his approach is anything but modular.

16 Stair, *Institutions*, I, 10, 3.

17 Ibid., I, 10, 4; 6.

18 As Lloyd and Stein each observe, until relatively recently throughout Europe 'a university trained lawyer was first and foremost a Roman lawyer': Howell A. Lloyd (trs.), 'Introduction' in *François Hotman: Antitribonian* (Brill, 2021), at 11.

19 Even learned Common lawyers, though, were generally afforded some knowledge of the *Institutes* of Gaius and Justinian, providing if not a map, at least the idea that law might be mapped: Birks, 'Definition and Division', at 1–2.

20 Gaius, *Institutes*, 3.88.

21 Ibid.: *quarum summa diuisio in duas species diducitur: omnis enim obligatio uel ex contractu nascitur uel ex delicto.*

22 Justinian, *Institutes*, 3.13.2.

23 Birks, 'Definition and Division', 18.

24 Note that where Gaius speaks of *obligationes ex delicto*, Justinian's *Institutes* prefers the formulation of *obligationes ex maleficio et ex quasi maleficio*: Justinian, *Institutes*, 3.13.2. Note, too, that in Justinian's *Institutes*, the 'principal division' of obligations is said to be between two *genera* (not *species*): Praetorian and Civil obligations (Justinian, *Institutes*, 3.13.2). The division between Praetorian and Civil obligations has been recognised as mapping onto the English divide between 'common law' and 'equitable' obligations (see Birks, 'Definition and Division', 13), but this divide has never been known to Scots law.

25 Indeed, 'some 1750 years [after Gaius] and a lot of legal history later, English law was still clinging to the view' that the divide between contract and tort was not merely *summa divisio obligationes*, but in fact *solae divisio obligationes*: Ibid., at 18. See also *Sinclair v. Brougham* [1914] AC 398, at 415 *per* Lord Chancellor Haldane.

26 See Nikolaos A. Davrados, *Restating the Civil Law of Quasi-Contract: Negotiorum Gestio and Unjust Enrichment*, [2023] J. Civil L. Stud. 1, 3.

27 Within Scotland, the unloved fourth category retains 'currency mainly to its use by the writer George Joseph Bell in his *Principles of the Law of Scotland*': see W.M. Gordon, 'Roman Quasi-Delicts and Scots Law' in *Roman Law, Scots Law and Legal History: Selected Essays* (Edinburgh University Press, 2007), 148; Bell, *Principles of the Law of Scotland* (2nd edn) (Blackwood, 1830), at 543, 553. It has been said, recently, by MacQueen to be wholly obsolete: MacQueen, *MacQueen and Thomson*, para.1.18.

28 That is, if they engage with the *Institutions* at all: As Wilson observed, the 'national focus' of the work, like other comparable commentaries, was such as to exclude an international audience, with the net effect that 'treatises by even the most celebrated of jurists were largely ignored by their contemporaries in other countries, who often had neither the ability to read nor the knowledge to comment upon these works of local or national law': Adelyn Wilson, *Stair and the Inleydinge of Grotius*, [2010] Edin. L. R. 259, 261.

29 Birks, 'Definition and Division', 28.

30 Such is not to say that the categories of 'contract' and 'delict' – or 'reparation' – were for Stair inconsequential, but rather that in his account they are not the supreme governing categories of 'obligations'.

31 *MacFarlane v. Johnston* (1864) 2M. 1210.

32 Stair, *Institutions*, I, 10, 3.

33 Hence, Stair himself in fact distinguishes here between 'obligations' and 'contracts' (Stair, *Institutions*, I, 10, 5) since the latter are necessarily *διπλευρος* ['two-sided']. The *Thesaurus Juris Civilis* suggests that obligations arising from *negotiorum gestio* are, like contractual obligations, *διπλευρος* ['two-sided'] – and this is consistent with the Roman law *per* (e.g.) D.3.5.2 (Gaius), but here *διπλευρος* cannot be read as synonymous with 'mutual', which is notable as 'mutuality' does mark out the unique feature of 'contracts' in Scots law. There seems, then, to be disparity between the word *διπλευρος* used in a more literal sense (i.e. as simply involving two persons) and the more particular sense used by Stair in this context (see *Thesaurus Juris Civilis* (H. W. Meyer, 1717), at 136). Note, also, that the reading of *διπλευρος* as akin to 'mutual' can still be made to work within the context of the *Thesaurus*, if *negotiorum gestio* is conceptualised as a species of *quasi*-contract, as on this basis the obligation in *negotiorum gestio* should be understood as a response to the *gestor*'s obligated act. This reading does not make sense in Stair's philosophy (Stair, of course, famously rejects the Roman quadripartite division in favour of his bipartite divide of *ex voluntate* and *ex lege* (I, 3, 2), however, nor does it fit within Scots law more broadly, where *negotiorum gestio* is not understood as a species of *quasi*-contract, but rather an independent *ex lege* obligation imposed 'without necessity of recurring to the strained supposition of a contract': see *Lord Kames' Principles of Equity* at 118(a). Nonetheless, being that *negotiorum gestio* – involves two claims (the *actio negotiorum gestio contraria* possessed by the *gestor* and the *actio negotiorum gestio directa* possessed by the *dominus*), the concept may be described as *διπλευρος*, but it cannot be described as mutual, since the claims may be exclusive of one another, and they are not interrelated or mutually dependent as those under a contract may be.

34 Stair, *Institutions*, I, 10, 5. Stair himself does not use this terminology, although he makes use of the Greek words *μονόπλευρος* ['one-sided'] and *διπλευρος* ['two-sided']. In context, it can be read that *μονόπλευρος* denotes an 'obligation' in which only one party stands as debtor, with the other standing as creditor. An 'obligation' which is *διπλευρος*, by contrast, is necessarily a contractual obligation and involves both, or all, parties to the obligation standing in a relationship which places burdens – which may or may not be interrelated (and so may or may not be truly 'mutual' in the sense of being interdependent) – on all involved, and is constituted by the consent of all involved (see Hogg, *Law and Language*, 227–228, 239–241). Though the burdens may be interrelated, the parties need not be burdened with the same duties or be burdened to the same extent; one party may be burdened with onerous duties, while the other is bound to do no more than accept the other party's performance: see *MacQueen and Thomson*, para.3.28.

35 Reinhard Zimmermann, *The Law of Obligations: Roman Foundations of the Civilian Tradition* (Oxford University Press, 1990), 1.

36 See Hogg, *Law and Language*, 130–131.

37 *I.e.*, where contracts are concerned, both parties are obliged to render performance to the other and both parties are entitled to demand performance from the other

– even if the 'performance' in question amounts to nothing more than acceptance of the others' performance.

38 This idea of a juristic, or juridical, act maps on to the German concept called *'Rechtsgeschäfte'*: Hogg, *Law and Language*, 131.

39 Stair, *Institutions*, I, 10, 6.

40 What is here styled a 'gratuitous contract' (see *MacQueen and Thomson*, para.3.28) imperfectly (imperfectly because consideration is not a necessary element for the creation of any contract in Scots law) maps on to the Common law concept of a 'unilateral contract' – that is, one in which there is a considerable disparity in the 'distribution of the obligational burden' between the parties to the contract. In other words, a 'gratuitous contract' should be understood as one in which only one party need to perform anything onerous (in the sense of burdensome), the other being expected to do no more than accept the corresponding obligant's performance. It should be stressed here that the language of 'unilateral contract[s]' ought to be rejected wholesale by Scots lawyers; this terminology is confusing and does not even accurately describe the operation of the law within the Common law tradition. In Scotland, the concept of bi- or multilaterality can and ought to be taken to denote the number of juridical acts or actors required to bring about a legal consequence (e.g. the conclusion of a marriage, creation of a contract or creation of a delictual obligation). Discussion of, or comparison to, the Anglo-American concept of a 'unilateral contract' is profoundly unhelpful and has no place in Scots law. Even if a contract involves such a considerable disparity in the 'distribution of the obligational burden' that a Common lawyer would be minded to style it a 'unilateral contract', such classification should be avoided since a so-called 'unilateral contract' is still fundamentally a 'contract', meaning that it is constituted by a combination of bi- or multilateral juridical acts and resultantly involves mutual, interdependent obligation(s) on both sides: See Hogg, *Law and Language*, 131 and the discussion below.

41 An obligation to assent to the receipt of something like money is quite different from an obligation to assent to the receipt of a white elephant – or some less metaphorical *damnosa donum* [ruinous gift] – *MacQueen and Thomson*, para.3.28.

42 *McNeill v. Aberdeen City Council (No.2)* [2013] CSIH 102, para.20.

43 Stair, *Institutions*, I, 10, 3.

44 While the former two conditions may be thought 'casual' (in that the fulfilment of the condition is not within the power of the beneficiary of the obligation, but rather a matter of chance), the last of these three hypothetical conditions is evidently potestative: that is to say, the fulfilment (or otherwise) of the condition is in the hands of the prospective beneficiary (see *MacQueen and Thomson*, para.4.69). In other words, while the conditions of a promise to do something on the birth of a child, or on that child's attainment of a certain age, can be met – or frustrated – without active effort on the part of the child in question, the prospective beneficiary of a promise of reward for finding a missing pet must proactively seek to fulfil the condition, and succeed in this attempt, to benefit from the promised reward. Unlike where suspensive conditions in contract law are concerned, being that the prospective beneficiary of a promise need not render acceptance to – or even be aware of – the stipulations of the promise, there is no duty on the part of a prospective beneficiary to realise a potestative promissory condition; this is distinct from the position in respect of contract law, where on the basis of the principle of mutuality of contract

'as a general rule, where [...] it appears that both parties have agreed that something shall be done, which cannot effectually be done unless both parties concur in doing it, the construction of the contract is that each agree to do all that is necessary to be done on his part': *MacKay v. Dick and Stephenson* (1881) 8 R. (HL) 37, at 40 *per* Lord Blackburn.

45 Ibid., I, 10, 5.

46 *MacQueen and Thomson*, para.4.63.

47 Stair, *Institutions*, I, 10, 3.

48 'All legal concepts must be formulated in words. The link between law and language is thus intimate and properly the subject of study in its own right [...] lawyers, it seems, don't mean what they say, a point some lawyers admit [...]. That the law appears to be couched in a foreign language, a language only the initiated can decipher, may be one of the reasons for the general dislike of lawyers': Ross G. Anderson, 'Introduction' in George Watson (ed.), *Bell's Dictionary and Digest of the Law of Scotland* (Edinburgh Legal Education Trust, 2012), at v.

49 For 'fundamental structural language' generally, see Hogg, *Law and Language*, at 1–11.

50 It should be stressed only in part; as Sellar observed, 'this entire area of law has been bedevilled by ambiguous and confusing terminology, exacerbated further in Scotland when the clarity of Stair was followed by the confusion of later writers': W. David H. Sellar, 'Promise' in Kenneth Reid and Reinhard Zimmermann, *A History of Private Law in Scotland: Volume 2: Obligations* (Oxford University Press, 2000), at 281.

51 See, generally, Eric Descheemaeker, *Mapping the Common Law: On a Recent English Attempt and Its Links with Scottish Jurisprudence*, [2003] Jur. Rev. 295.

52 Burrows, *Obligations*, at 2.

53 Antoine Berman, 'La traduction et la lettre – ou l'auberge du lointain' in Antoine Berman (ed.), *Les Tours de Babel: Essais sur la Traduction* (Mauzevin, 1985), 36–37.

54 See, generally, Leslie Dodd, 'Introduction' in *Jus Feudale Tribus Libris Comprehensum*, Volume II (Stair Society, 2025).

55 Hogg, *Law and Language*, at 305.

56 Stair is quite fond of listing synonyms for the key conceptual words that he employs, as where he equates 'rights personal' with 'obligations' (later, as noted above, contrasting 'obligations' with 'contracts'), before subsequently noting that from the debtor's perspective a personal right is seen as an 'Obligation, Debt, or Duty' (Stair, *Institutions*, I, 2, 1).

57 See Martin Hogg, *Promise: The Neglected Obligation in European Private Law*, [2010] International and Comparative Law Quarterly 461.

58 Hogg, *Law and Language, passim.*

59 Jonathan Brown, *Medical Intervention and Incapax Patients: The Place of* Negotiorum Gestio *within Law's 'Fundamental Structural Language'*, [2022] Edin. L. R. 422, 422.

60 Ibid.

61 Hogg, *Law and Language*, 10.

62 Ibid., 131.

63 Ibid., 141.

64 Ibid., 139.

65 See *Petition of George Logan, Lastmaker, and Late Bailie of Canongate*, 3 July 1747, in the collection of the Bodleian Library, Oxford, at 3. The term is a portmanteau of the Greek *μονόπλευρος* (utilised by Stair) and the post-Justinianic Latin *unilateralis.*

Μονόπλευρος and *unilateralis* were employed as synonyms of one another for a time, though as discussed *infra* equation of the modern English term 'unilateral' with *μονόπλευρος* is problematic, since the counterpart of *μονόπλευρος* – *δίπλευρος* – does not map on to the English-language term 'bilateral', but rather 'mutual/reciprocal'.
66 Ibid., 145.
67 *Replies of Gavin Ralston, Defender, to the Answers of George Earl of Crawfurd, Pursuer*, 9 December 1762, Bodleian Library Collection, Oxford, 9.
68 Kenneth G.C. Reid, *From Text-Book to Book of Authority: The Principles of George Joseph Bell*, [2011] Edin. L. R. 6, 6.
69 This, of course, is entirely consistent with the fact that 'institutional writers are essentially textbook writers and commentators and their works are supposed to be principally descriptive': See Rahmatian, *The Role of Institutional Writers in Scots Law*.
70 Hogg, *Law and Language*, 146.
71 Ibid., 133.
72 Ibid.
73 Ibid., 227.
74 Dig.3.5.2 (Gaius): No single Latin word, akin to either *δίπλευρος*, or 'two-sided' or 'mutual', is used in this Pandect: rather, the wording is more literally 'on the one side and on the other'.
75 Recall, however, that *δίπλευρος* does not, in all cases, map on to the notion of 'mutuality'.
76 Ibid., 193.
77 Ibid.
78 Ibid., 194.
79 Ibid., 203.
80 Ibid.
81 Bankton, *Institute*, I, 9, 1.
82 Hogg, *Law and Language*, 203.
83 Used here in the sense of authoritative juridical 'declaration', of which see Peter Stein, *Regulae Iuris: From Juristic Rules to Legal Maxims* (Edinburgh University Press, 1966), 9–19.
84 This is a modification of what Hogg terms 'sense two' of the term: Hogg, *Law and Language*, 181. The omission of 'hope of' is necessary because even in those cases in which something is given in the absence of any expectation of benefit or reciprocation, the party bound to give may harbour a hope of some (perhaps intangible) benefit; in other words, a gratuitous obligation may be constituted by one who hopes for delayed gratification.
85 Ibid., 181.
86 Joe Thomson, *Promises and the Requirements of Writing*, [1997] SLT (News) 284, 284.
87 Whether the obligation comes into being by way of unilateral undertaking (promise) or bilateral agreement (contract) is immaterial.
88 The term 'transaction' can, here, be read in the broad sense with which it is ascribed by s.9 of the Age of Legal Capacity (Scotland) Act 1991. For an example of an enforceable obligation arising out of a situation akin to this, see *Robertson v. Anderson* 2003 SLT 235.
89 This view, it is submitted, is consistent with the opinion of Lord Drummond Young (delivering a *per curiam* judgement) in *Van Klaveren v. Servisair UK Ltd* 2009 SLT 576.

Therein, at para.9, the court found that a 'unilateral obligation is normally gratuitous', thus implying, naturally, that it need not necessarily be so.

90 See, e.g., Hector L. MacQueen, [1986] SLT (News) 1, at 2; Stair Memorial Encyclopaedia, *Obligations*, Volume 15, para.613.

91 Consider the view of Lord President Gill expressed in *Regus Maxim Ltd. v. Bank of Scotland Plc* [2013] CSIH 12 at para.34: 'a promise places an obligation on the promisor and on no one else. It may result in the promisor's being given something in return, typically where the promise is made subject to a condition; but the promise does not oblige the promisee to fulfil the condition.'

92 Stair, *Institutions*, I, 10, 1.

93 Ibid., I, 10, 2.

94 Ibid., I, 10, 1.

95 William W. McBryde, *Promises in Scots Law*, [1993] ICLQ 48, 56.

96 Indeed, explicit reference to Stair's typology of 'acts of the will' was made by Lord President Hamilton in *Cawdor v. Cawdor*, 2007 SC 285, para.15.

97 Stair, *Institutions*, I, 10, 2.

98 The stages of 'desire', 'resolution' and 'engagement' can – as Ward and Curk note – be conceptualised as sequential or successive: Adrian D. Ward and Polona Curk, *Respecting 'Will': Viscount Stair and Online Shopping*, [2018] SLT (News) 123, at 125. 'That these are separate steps is shown in cases where a volitional impairment may prevent engagement', the authors note, citing *Ward, Appellant* 2014 S.L.T. (Sh Ct) 15.

99 'Resolution' does necessarily involve an extrinsic expression on the part of the resolver; that is to say, that unlike desire – which is uncommunicated – the fact of the resolver's 'resolution' may be made known to others, including the prospective creditor(s) in the obligation. Nonetheless, even with this knowledge on the part of a prospective creditor – and even with proof of 'a resolution exprest both by word and write' – no obligation is created, albeit that given that 'matter [which a resolution concerns may] be necessar, or that the resolution be holden forth to assure others: the alteration whereof, without evident ground, importeth levity and inconstancy, and sometimes deceit and unfaithfulness', it is possible that the general principles of personal bar may be invoked to prevent a resolver from advancing an argument that their expression of will was merely 'resolution'. Indeed, this was the rationale for the operation of the 'postal acceptance rule' seemingly given by Lord Fullerton in the Inner House case of *Dunlop v. Higgins* (1847) 9 D. 1413 (at 1422), though his opinion was rejected on appeal to the House of Lords. For personal bar generally, see Elspeth C. Reid and John W.G. Blackie, *Personal Bar* (W. Green, 2006).

100 Stair, *Institutions*, I, 10, 2, citing *Kincaid v. Dickson* [1673] Mor 12143.

101 Ibid.

102 See, e.g., *Harvey v. Facey* [1893] AC 552; *Fisher v. Bell* [1961] 1 Q.B 394. *Pharmaceutical Society of Great Britain v Boots Cash Chemists* [1953] 1 QB 410 provides an example of 'resolution' in action in the English courts, and the facts of that case broadly map on to the practical description of the nature of 'resolution' given by Ward and Curk in their 2018 article on Stair's theory of obligations: 'The shopper is attracted by various items (desire), and decides to purchase some by adding them to the basket (resolution). But to complete the operation of the will to purchase the items, the shopper has to commit with a further act, that is, pay for them (engagement). Without this final act [...] the shopper will abandon the whole process: the will is not efficacious.' See Ward and Curk, *Respecting 'Will'*, 125.

103 Hugh Beale (ed.), *Chitty on Contracts* (35th edn), Volume 1 (Sweet and Maxwell, 2023), para.4.011.

104 Stair, *Institutions*, I, 10, 2.

105 Ibid., I, 10, 4.

106 As manifestly demonstrated in *Petrie v. Earl of Airlie* (1834) 13 S. 68, a case concerning promise of reward that pre-dates the infamous English case of *Carlill v. Carbolic Smoke Ball Co.* [1893] 1 QB 256 by over half a century, and resolved the dispute without any reference to the strained supposition of a contract. Contrast *Chitty on Contracts*, para.4.007.

107 Notably, the identifiable subject need not be a 'person', or even exist, at the time that the obligation is created: See Jonathan Brown, *Jus Quaesitum Tertio: A Res, Not A Right?* [2017] Jur. Rev. 53, 54.

108 Stair, *Institutions*, I, 1, 20.

109 Ibid., I, 5, 7.

110 Ibid., I, 9, 2–4.

111 Ibid., I, 7, 2.

112 Ibid., I, 8, 2.

113 This idea is given concrete expression by (then-Lord President) Hope in *Lord Advocate v. Glasgow City Council* (1990) SLT 721, 725.

114 Stair, *Institutions*, I, 10, 7.

115 [1631] Mor 15562.

116 Stair, *Institutions*, I, 10, 7.

117 [2013] CSIH 12, para.37.

118 The notion that deeds, rather than words, may create a binding unilateral obligation is controverted at present, with contradictory authority from the Outer House in spite of Lord Gill's unequivocal judgement in *Regus Maxim*. Lord Malcolm – in *Fisher v. Applied Drilling Technology* [2016] CSOH 108 – appeared to countenance the possibility of an implied promise, while on the same day Lord Bannatyne in *Landvest PCC Ltd. v. Cushley and ors.* [2016] CSOH 109 described, at para.26, 'the law applicable to unilateral promissory obligations [...] as as set out in *Regis (Maxim) Ltd v Bank of Scotland PLC*'. For academic discussion of binding unilateral obligations arising through implication, see Jonathan Brown, *On Promises, Partnership and Succession*, [2023] Jur. Rev. 121.

119 Section 11 (1) of this legislation provides that 'the rule of law by which a person who is not a party to a contract may acquire a right to enforce or otherwise invoke the contract's terms does not apply in relation to contracts constituted on or after the day this section comes into force', radically departing from the position expressed by Stair and so Scots Common law.

120 Stair, *Institutions*, I, 10, 5.

121 Ibid. It should be noted that a several promise to the benefit of a third party can also be made by one of the two contracting parties, who will be bound by this several unilateral obligation: *per* Lord Malcolm 'Scots law will enforce a unilateral undertaking that is intended to have legal effect, notwithstanding an absence of consideration. Such an undertaking may, but need not be, collateral to a separate contract, and will be subject to an objective test, *i.e.*, that which a reasonable outside observer would infer from all the circumstances': *Fisher v. Applied Drilling Technology* [2016] CSOH 108 at para.26. This position may have been modified by s.11 (1) of the Contract (Rights of Third Parties) (Scotland) Act 2017, but it is unclear.

122 Ibid., I, 10, 6.
123 For the significance of 'functional', as opposed to 'linguistic' equivalence, see *Ted Jacobs Engineering Group Ltd. v. Johnston Marshall and Partners* [2014] CSIH 18, para.90, *per* Lord Drummond Young.
124 *Chitty on Contracts*, para.1.050.
125 Hogg, *Perspectives*, 651: 'the idea of an exchange would have been unhelpful for Stair, as his treatment of contract sets out the Scottish rule that gratuitous contracts are as equally enforceable as onerous ones, there being no rule of mutual exchange or consideration'.
126 Ibid.
127 Bogle, *Contract*, at 71.
128 McBryde, *Contract Law in Scotland*, para.6–110.
129 D. Neil MacCormick, *Institutions of Law* (Oxford University Press, 2007).
130 Brown, *Jus Quaesitum Tertio.*
131 Hogg, *Tricky Problems*, [1997] SLT (News) 25, 28–29.
132 Ibid., at 28.
133 Ibid.
134 Stair Memorial Encyclopaedia, *Obligations*, Volume 15, para.613.
135 McBryde, *Contract*, para.2.33.
136 1911 S.C. 103.
137 Ibid., at 111.
138 In other words, they are not 'events', in the sense discussed by Birks: of which see 'Definition and Division'.
139 McBryde, *Contract*, para.2.33.
140 Ibid.
141 Such, it is submitted, is consistent with the opinion of Lord Kinnear as expressed in *Morton's Trustees v. The Aged Christian Friend Society of Scotland* (1899) 2 F 82, 85.
142 *Regus Maxim Ltd. v. Bank of Scotland Plc* [2013] CSIH 12, para.34.
143 *Cawdor v Cawdor* [2007] CSIH 3, para.15.
144 That is to say, its essentially bilateral and mutual nature, in terms of the fundamental structural language discussed above.
145 *Regus Maxim* para.34. It should be stressed here that just as communication is immaterial for 'promise' and 'acceptance', so too should it taken to be immaterial where extant offers are withdrawn. The fact that an offer requires communication to the offeree for its acceptance to be possible is more a matter of brute physical fact than of legal principle; one cannot accept an offer if one does not know that the offer is on the table. If it is recognised that an offer – as an act of engagement – may be withdrawn without effective communication of the withdrawal, then the difficulties identified by the Lord President in *Thomson v. James* (1855) 18 D. 1 at 10–11 can be avoided.
146 *Bogie (t/a Oakbank Services) v. The Forestry Commission* 2002 SCLR 278, para.27 *per* Lord MacFadyen.
147 *Glasgow Steam Shipping Co. v. Watson* (1873) 1 R. 189; *Wylie and Lochhead v. McElroy and Sons* (1873) 1 R. 41.
148 Bell, *Commentaries*, 327.
149 Requirements of Writing (Scotland) Act 1995, s.1 (1).
150 At para.15.
151 Consider George L. Gretton, *Missives by Fax or Pdf?* [2010] Edin. L. R. 280, 281–282.

152 [1955] 2 QB 327. This, of course, goes against the position suggested by *MacQueen and Thomson*, para.2.47.

153 See *Cawdor v. Cawdor* SC 285.

154 Hector L. MacQueen, 'The Law of Obligations in Scots Law' in Reiner Schulze and Fryderyk Zoll (eds), *The Law of Obligations in Europe: A New Wave of Codifications* (Sellier European Law Publishers, 2013), at 215.

155 As McBryde notes, 'offer and acceptance [...] should not be regarded as the necessary form of every contract' (McBryde, *Contract*, para.6-05) and indeed MacQueen has noted that what McBryde terms the 'master concept' – conceptualised by McBryde and MacQueen alike as 'agreement', but in rationalisable in Stair's taxonomy as effective engagement – 'allow[ed] the reintroduction of counterpart execution in Scots law by statute in 2015 without any sense of creeping Anglicisation' (Hector L. MacQueen, 'Its in the Post! Distance Contracting in Scotland 1681–1855' in Frankie MacCarthy, James Chalmers and Stephen Bogle (eds), *Essays in Conveyancing and Property Law in Honour of Professor Robert Rennie* (Open Book Publishers, 2015), 71). Naturally, it may be submitted that such legislation would not, in fact, have been needed had the Scottish courts paid proper mind to precedent and Stair's philosophy.

156 See *Carlyle v. Royal Bank of Scotland* [2015] UKSC 13, at para.35.

157 Ward and Curk, *Respecting 'Will'*; see also Hogg, *Perspectives*, 651.

158 As Professor Gretton observed in reflecting on his own *festschrift*, 'One type of mediocre legal scholarship is the mere accumulation of data; one type of mediocre legal teaching is the mere serving-up of data like limp fried eggs on a hotel breakfast hotplate. And there is another type of mediocre teaching and scholarship: all nebulous theory, of no use to God or man.' Stair's *Institutions*, by this metric, are anything but mediocre.

159 See Paton, 'Institutions', 201.

160 As Professor Clive observed, 'it may be an exaggeration to say that there is nothing so practical as a good theory [...] a good set of tools [may be] of more practical value. But [...] a good theory can indeed be of some practical value': Eric Clive, 'Nothing So Practical as a Good Theory: The Notion of a Requirement' in Andrew J.M. Steven, Ross G. Anderson and John MacLeod, *Nothing So Practical as a Good Theory: Festschrift for George L. Gretton* (Avizandum, 2017), 53.

161 This statement is of general application, but can be concretised in the context of this chapter by considering the issues relating to the 'accepted promise' discussed above, as well as the fact that, despite being consistent with the principles espoused in Stair, the cases of *Smith v. Duke of Gordon* (1701) Mor. 16987, as well as *Cubbison v. Cubbison* (1716) Mor. 16988, seem 'so surprising at first sight'. 'For two centuries, [Scots] lawyers [have] been taught that a contract was created by an offer by one party met by an acceptance by another [...] but the doctrines associated with offer and acceptance, painfully learned by generations of law students and applied with variable degrees of success in tackling tutorial and examination problems, do not appear to have been at the forefront of the Scots law on contract formation in general before 1800' – MacQueen, 'Distance Contracting', 48–49.

162 MacQueen, for his part, suggests that 'Bell's positions on [questions of formation of voluntary obligations, as adapted from Stair] failed to last as the law of Scotland, however' citing the case of *Countess of Dunmore v. Alexander* (1830) 9 S 190 as positive authority for this proposition – in spite of the fact that the House of Lords decision in

Dunlop v. Higgins (1848) 1 HLC 381 quite expressly affirmed the validity of Bell's – and so Stair's – view. Rather than the law 'changing', it is here submitted that the issues that have emerged in Scots jurisprudence since the mid-nineteenth century onwards have largely arisen from misinterpretation and misunderstanding and so should be thought open to juridical correction, without any necessary need for legislative intervention (i.e. if the law has 'changed' as a result of misunderstandings, it should be open for these changes to be reverted and a return to principle facilitated).

163 Of course, it is possible that English jurisprudence may develop in such a way as to reject the idea of the 'postal rule' as an exception of 'convenience' (see *Chitty on Contracts*, para.4.079) and instead come to adhere to the view that engagement concludes and creates obligations (including contracts). Such, however, would perhaps necessitate the first step(s) being taken by the Scottish courts and jurisprudents – a line of development which would be prematurely smothered by s.4 of the Contract (Formation) (Scotland) Bill.

164 Douglas Brodie, *Pursuing the Police and Assumption of Responsibility: Tindall v Chief Constable of Thames Valley*, [2022] Jur. Rev. 100, 104.

165 Consider *Thomson v. James* (1855) 18 D. 1, which directly considers the question of 'postal acceptance' with reference to Stair's *Institutions* and theory of will.

166 Neither Lord Ormidale in *Burnley v. Alford* 1909 SLT 123 nor Lord Kirkwood in *MacMillan v. Caldwell* 1990 SC 389 cite or discuss Stair, Bell or the basic principles of voluntary obligation creation in their judgements, preferring discussion of positive precedent (including from the English Chancery Court in *Burnley*) only. In *Verdin Brothers v. Robertson* (1871) 10 M. 35, there was 'a glimmer of recognition of the notion of apparent consent [but ultimately] the judges were content to resolve the problem of the mutilated telegram with reference to English precedent represented by *Henkel v. Pape* (1870) LR 6 Exch 7': Lubbe, 'Formation of Contract', at 38.

167 Gloag, for instance, suggests that 'of the theories propounded to account for this rule [...] the most coherent is that the offerer [*sic*] must be taken as impliedly contracting to treat a letter posted as an acceptance and notification to him', citing the English case of *Byrne v. Van Tienhoven* 1880 5 CPD 344 (*Contract*, at 34). This preference for Common law precedent over Scots law principle is regrettable, and the present author must – like T.B. Smith – admit to a preference for sharing the stake with Stair rather than glory with Gloag. Even Smith himself falls foul of failing to consider Stair, however. In his *Short Commentary*, Smith stresses the 'Civilian' nature of Scots law, omitting consideration of Stair and his typology of obligations in the chapter on 'formation and content of contracts' (754–772). Interestingly, the French jurist Pothier – so influential on nineteenth-century English legal thought – is instead cited by Smith (at fn.3, p.755).

Chapter 2

THE 'POSTAL ACCEPTANCE RULE': PROFOUNDLY UNEXCEPTIONAL

Introduction

The so-called 'postal acceptance rule' – which, to reiterate, describes the phenomenon whereby the simple physical posting of an acceptance to the offeror, not the receipt of said acceptance by said offeror, is taken to be the point at which a contract is formed[1] – is conceptualised as an exception to the general rule that an acceptance must be communicated to an offeror for a contract to be created.[2] This analysis of the phenomenon seems to fit well enough within the framework of English law,[3] wherein the idea of a nominate 'postal acceptance rule' emerged and has been recognised since the nineteenth century.[4] In English contract law, it ostensibly makes sense to regard the apparent rule as an exception to the general position that there must be effective communication of the terms of any bargain for that bargain to be enforceable.[5] Anglo-American contract law is just that: a law of contract, in other words a topic-heading concerning the regulation of enforceable agreements underpinned by consideration.[6] Essentially, the formation of any contract *qua* contract is (minimally) a two-way process involving direct communication between two persons. For one to bind the other to a contract without that other's knowledge or active consent seems *ex facie* exceptional, if not simply impossible.

The idea of there existing a discrete 'postal acceptance rule' has appeared in Scots law,[7] as well as English law. As indicated in the introduction to this book, the nature of the Scots rule has hitherto been conceptualised by academics – and by some (though certainly not all judges)[8] – as being essentially the same in this jurisdiction as it is in the Common law world. That is to say, it is generally thought that the 'postal acceptance rule' exists as an exceptional quirk of the Victorian age which should – ideally – be excised from the law as 'out of keeping' with modern life in the twenty-first century.[9] This chapter, by contrast, posits that the conceptualisation of the 'postal acceptance rule' as an exception is in Scots law – whatever the position may be in the Common law world – fundamentally incorrect. Instead of being in any way 'exceptional', the 'postal acceptance rule' is in fact nothing more than a manifestation of the ordinary rules pertaining to the creation of voluntary obligations in this jurisdiction.[10] The mistaken belief that the Scots 'postal acceptance rule' is in any way exceptional has arisen from a culture which has come to regard Scotland as being in possession, simply, of a 'law of contract' akin to the English equivalent.[11] As was made plain in the previous chapter, this is not in fact the case.[12] Rather, the principles which underpin the Scots law of voluntary obligations, as articulated by Stair though further adapted – as is discussed by this chapter by Stair's juristic successor, Bell – essentially ensures as a matter of logical necessity that it is the 'act of acceptance which, in the language of Mr Bell in his Commentaries, "binds the bargain"' rather than the communication thereof.[13]

By taking the view that there exists a discrete and nominate 'postal acceptance rule' which is amenable to abolition, the SLC can consequently be taken to have made an essential category error in its conceptualisation of the present Scots law pertaining to formation of obligations. Accordingly, this chapter seeks to make the case that – particularly given that the proposed abrogation of 'any rule of law whereby, in relation to the formation of a contract, an acceptance sent by means of a postal service takes effect when posted'[14] is unquestionably radical – there is cause to consider caution in introducing sweeping changes to the essential fabric of Scots private law by legislative fiat. Properly understood, the 'postal acceptance rule' is not an aberration in this jurisdiction, but rather a concretised manifestation of the applied principles of jurisprudence.

As was recognised by the Lord Ordinary in the case of *Jacobsen Sons & Co v. Underwood & Sons Ltd.*,[15] the view expressed by Bell that the 'act' of 'acceptance "binds the bargain"', rather than the communication thereof, 'is not limited to the case of an acceptance despatched by post',[16] albeit that (particularly in the context of the nineteenth century) it has most readily found practical expression in that context. In the age of digital and instantaneous communication, particularly digital and instantaneous communication which does not leave some 'principal' document in the hands of the sender,[17] it is thought that Scots lawyers have more to learn from their own legal history and jurisprudence than from particular decisions reached by courts from outwith the jurisdiction, in respect of a fundamentally distinct system of 'contracting'. Consequently, given that it is recognised that the SLC's draft bill 'is brief and does not provide all the answers to' a panoply of questions concerning 'communicat[ion] in the digital age',[18] it is thought that detailed consideration of the present law relating to 'acceptance' within the schema developed by Stair and refined by Bell is warranted. By seeking to prioritise 'communication' of acceptance over 'engagement' signifying will to be bound,[19] the SLC would appear to be suggesting a far more radical overhaul of the Scots law of voluntary obligations than they *ex facie* appear to in their various reports. The present author takes the view that such an overhaul would be undesirable, although of course on grounds of policy other opinions may be held. Nonetheless, in advance of any such overhaul, a full and frank discussion of what may be lost if a fundamental 'break with the existing tradition' of Scots jurisprudence is legislatively effected.[20]

Consequently, though the position that 'there is no good reason to privilege postal over other forms of acceptance', expressed by the SLC,[21] seems eminently sensible, it is here submitted that (whatever the position may be south of the Tweed or in the wider Common law world) the principles of Scots law do not in fact appear to do so. Rather, there presently exists the potential for the law to develop, judicially, to expressly recognise that the act of sending an acceptance via text message, or email or any other form of instant digital communication, 'binds the bargain', regardless of what may have been decided by courts from outwith the jurisdiction. That this has not, as yet, occurred can be attributed to the fact that the 'postal acceptance rule' has come to be seen as a discrete and ossified anomaly. This chapter, consequently, seeks to establish that the 'postal acceptance rule' is in fact far from exceptional. Rather, it simply describes, in shorthand, the consequence of the profoundly unexceptional application of the basic principles of Scots voluntary obligations law.

The 'Reception of' the 'Postal Acceptance Rule'

The 'postal acceptance rule', which is sometimes referred to as the 'dispatch rule',[22] is generally said to have been introduced into English law by the 1818 case of *Adams v. Lindsell*,[23] under the influence of Pothier's 'will theory'[24] of contract formation whereby 'a subjective meeting of minds sufficed to form a contract, regardless of the communication of those subjective wills'.[25] Stair's *Institutions* was first published some eighty years before Pothier's pioneering work, and it should be noted that although 'Stair has sometimes been viewed simplistically as supporting a wholly will based theory of contract law',[26] his thought is in fact the product of a more sophisticated blend of 'natural law [reason] and will approaches'.[27] Nonetheless, though Stair cannot be categorised as a 'pure will theorist', it may be posited that Stair and Pothier would align in agreeing that the act of posting a letter can be identified as 'engagement' signalling intention to be legally bound, so bringing into being a binding obligation.

The alignment of Stair and Pothier can be inferred through reference to the work of Bell, who lauded Stair and his 'admirable achievement' in writing the *Institutions*, 'so good in arrangement, so distinguished for sound judgment and excellent adaptation to the business and concerns of men, that it would seem almost beyond the age in which it was written', in the preface to his own *Commentaries*.[28] For his part, Bell has been – and not without reason – described as 'the greatest legal writer in Scotland next to Stair'.[29] In the *Commentaries*, he adopted and conformed to Stair's view of conventional obligations arising from acts of engagement[30] and, furthermore, cited Pothier extensively in the later editions of his principal works.[31] 'In both *Commentaries* and *Principles* [however,] Bell's earliest treatments relied almost entirely on Scottish case authorities'[32] and indeed it should be noted that 'the Civilian sources and authors chosen [by Bell] differ from book to book of the *Commentaries*'.[33] While Bell favoured Pothier in his discussion of partnership law, for instance, he is plain in his 'discussion of the standard of seaworthiness of a ship [that] Scots law was said to follow the views of Valin rather than Pothier'.[34]

Pothier is however cited, by Bell, at the outset of his chapter on the 'General Principles of Obligations and Contract', with 'the essence of every obligation' being defined as 'an engagement or undertaking to give or to do something, conferring on him to whom the engagement is undertaken a right of exacting performance'.[35] Indeed, it is this 'right of exacting performance' that is taken to be the underlying principle which justifies the view that specific implement is, in Scots law, the creditor's right, rather than a mere equitable remedy available only in limited circumstances.[36] This, consistent with the general principles of Scots jurisprudence, assures the primacy of the principle *pacta sunt servanda* and provides the underlying rationale for the Scottish courts' preference for ordering performance ahead of awards of substitutory[37] 'damages'.[38] Fundamentally, Bell follows Stair's approach to 'conventional' obligations closely (though he departs wildly from Stair's theology and his view of 'obediential' obligations),[39] emphasising that Scots law departs substantially from 'the elaborate divisions of the Civilians' in recognising a simpler divide between obligations voluntarily constituted and those imposed by law.[40] The focus of his treatment in the *Commentaries* is almost entirely on the former, with only limited discussion of the latter as they arise in a mercantile context (which is unsurprising, given the focus of his work).[41]

While Bell departs from Stair's overarching typology of 'obligations', this is principally because of his concern with mercantile – rather than general – jurisprudence. Accordingly, his focus, in the *Commentaries*, is on Conventional obligations and insofar as these are concerned he is unequivocal: 'in order to constitute a full and perfect obligation, there must, on the part of the obligor, be a deliberate consent and engagement to him who is to have the right of exacting performance'.[42] In assessing whether or not such 'deliberate consent' has been given, Bell refers to Stair's 'acts of the will' although unlike Stair (and perhaps again because of his principally mercantile focus) his account appears to be more on the giving of 'consent', and so there is greater focus on the achievement of 'agreement' than is present in Stair's *Institutions.* Notwithstanding this emphasis on 'contract' as opposed to *ex voluntate* obligations more generally, Bell does recognise that unilaterally constituted obligations are binding in Scots law, though – perhaps unsurprisingly – he does not, like Stair, expressly suggest that *omne verbum de ore fideli cadit in debitum.* Rather, his account is limited to unilateral obligations which may arise in a commercial context, such as 'bonds of cautionary or suretiship',[43] although it is implicitly acknowledged that any unilaterally constituted obligation 'to perform an act' will – subject to requirements of formality, capacity, legality, possibility and determinacy (as well as the requirement that the act in question not be *de minimis*)[44] – be enforceable.[45]

Given the nature of his work, Bell does not expressly draw any link between 'promise', 'offer' and 'acceptance' as species of engagement, although (confusingly, given his earlier adoption of Stair's typology) he does recognise that 'an offer is a resolution or engagement, provisional on acceptance, and as such proposed to the adverse party'.[46] Though the conflation of 'resolution' and 'engagement' seems self-contradictory and – indeed – may be charged with misleading those jurisprudents who considered his, and Stair's, work in dealing with questions of postal acceptance, it seems apparent from the context of Bell's account that offer is firmly understood as a species of 'engagement' in Stair's sense, rather than mere 'resolution'. Hence, 'the engagement should be so distinct and specific, that the party may be enabled at once to put his finger on it and say "here is my agreement" [...] an offer is necessarily under the condition of acceptance [...] by acceptance it becomes a contract; and this acceptance may be either in words, or by writing, or by doing what is required as the counterpart of the offer'.[47] 'Thus it appears that Bell, like Pothier, saw offer and acceptance as two concurrent declarations of the parties' wills with the acceptor not having to communicate acceptance to the offeror to make the contract binding'.[48] In this, Bell's view can be taken to accord with the positive law of Scotland as interpreted and applied by the courts in the early nineteenth century and before, as well as with the interpretative schema of natural justice espoused by Stair. To that end, then, it may be inferred that the 'postal acceptance' rule was not an exceptional doctrine received into Scotland following the case of *Adams v. Lindsell*,[49] rather *Adams* merely provided a case example from a distinct jurisdiction which can be rationalised in accordance with the general principles of Scots jurisprudence.[50]

Where Stair may be said, by Bogle, to have been 'unfortunately unclear',[51] Bell is unequivocal. In his own words (from the fifth edition of his work – the last published in his lifetime),[52] 'it is the act of acceptance that binds the bargain; and in the common case it is not necessary that the acceptance shall have reached the person who makes the offer'.[53] For Bell, the idea that an acceptance would not conclude a contract until it was received by the offeror was in fact exceptional; indeed, it was an exceptional circumstance that he envisaged with reference to a hypothetical case: 'From the moment of acceptance there is between the parties *in idem placitum concursus et conventio*, which constitutes the contract of sale. To this, however, an exception may be made by the offerer, limiting it so that the arrival of the acceptance only shall bind the bargain. Thus, a merchant in Leith offers 500 quarters of wheat to a merchant in London, at a certain price, receiving your answer at Leith in course.' He, by this form of answer, stipulates absolute freedom, if it should in any way happen, though by no fault or neglect of the other party, that the acceptance does not arrive by that post'.[54]

Per MacQueen, 'Bell's position [...] failed to last as the law of Scotland, however', with his (and so Stair's) views 'beg[inning] to run into difficulties in [Bell's] lifetime'[55] with the 1830 case of *Countess of Dunmore v. Alexander*.[56] This case, however, is 'not very satisfactory' and indeed in the later, and in many respects seminal, case of *Thomson v. James* was 'explained as being justifiable on its special facts – namely, that there had been a common agent and that the two letters could be read together, so that the second was in effect a postscript to the first'.[57] As such, it can be said that the case – and its result – is neither logical nor meaningfully predicated on legal principle; indeed, the majority of the court appear to depart from Bell's view (which had been endorsed by the Sheriff-Substitute at first instance)[58] without explanation or justification. Interestingly, even Lord Cragie, in dissent, appeared to hold the view that intimation of acceptance was necessary;[59] all four of the Session judges, then, were of a mind that communication of acceptance marked the completion of the contract rather than the simple act of 'engagement' demonstrating the offerees' intention to be legally bound.

Quite what led the court in *Countess of Dunmore* to this opinion 'is not completely clear'.[60] In the Outer House, Lord Newton appears to have considered Stair's *Institutions* (the work, however, was not quoted in argument) but ultimately formed the view that 'expression of consent to an unconnected third party' could not amount to engagement.[61] Rather than marking a radical departure from the principles of Scots law as espoused by Stair and Bell, however, it would instead appear that the court here sought to apply those principles, even if they ultimately did not do so satisfactorily. Consequently, though the case can be marked as indicating 'a move towards a requirement of communication between parties before statements of obligatory content could even begin to be considered binding or legally effective',[62] and the idea of this requirement has certainly been run with by academic commentators since the nineteenth century,[63] it is submitted that the centrality of 'communication' to contract formation is not in fact as fixed in Scots jurisprudence as has hitherto been conceived.[64] Certain nineteenth-century judges – notably Lord Fullerton[65] – adopted and promulgated the view that an offeree must know of acceptance for an obligation to be created,[66] but in addition to standing opposed to fundamental principle this view was expressly disavowed on appeal to the House of Lords in the 1848 case of *Dunlop v. Higgins*.[67]

When *Dunlop* called before the House of Lords, the Lord Chancellor noted that the proposition that an acceptance is deemed to conclude and create a contract on its posting 'has been so decided in cases in England, and none has been cited from Scotland which controverts that proposition', going on further to express his view that the cases in England put it [the question of the need for communication] beyond doubt'.[68] On the face of it, citing the English cases *Stocken v. Collen*[69] and *Adams v. Lindsell*,[70] it would appear that the Lord Chancellor was here engaged in little more than the sort of 'legal imperialism' which later Scots commentators, such as Walker, T. B. Smith and 'most polemically' by A. D. Gibb,[71] would bemoan and decry as being the perverse practice of the House of Lords in the nineteenth century.[72] Indeed, as the twin English cases were said to 'leave no doubt at all on the subject' for his Lordship, who perhaps unsurprisingly concluded that 'the law of Scotland appears to be the same as the law of England',[73] the possibility of decrying the judgement as one of enforced Anglicisation from an Imperial Common law court is manifest. Nonetheless, although the Lord Chancellor's decision is indeed principally predicated on English precedent – and his Lordship's proclamation concerning the parity of Scots and English law is certainly overstatement – it is here submitted that the view expressed in *Dunlop* is in fact consistent with the general principles of Scots law as espoused by Bell and Stair. Rather than standing as an act of aggressive Anglicisation, the judgement in fact reflects a principled application (if arrived at through unorthodox, if not then or now uncommon, means) of Scots law.[74]

Indeed, although no reference is made to Stair in the case, the Court did note that 'Bell's Commentary lays down the same rule [i.e., the English postal acceptance rule] as existing in Scotland', and while this formulation may be criticised (as it is not a particular 'postal acceptance rule' articulated by Bell, but rather a statement of general principle) it is indicative of the court's willingness to accept Bell's – and so Stair's – view of acts of 'engagement' as essential to the formation of voluntary obligations. As indicated, Bell, like Stair, identifies that the principal divide in the Scots law of obligations is between those conventional and obediential (i.e. *ex voluntate* and *ex lege*) and cites Stair's 'three acts of the will' as relevant to the formation of any obligation in Scots law.[75] Though the court in *Dunlop* expressly founds upon English case law as authority for the 'postal acceptance rule', it consequently appears that the decision in *Dunlop* is in fact consistent with the general principles of Scots obligations law and is not indicative of any move away from the norms described in Stair's *Institutions*. As such, it cannot be said that the 'postal acceptance rule' was positively received into Scots law from English, or by virtue of the authority or particular persuasiveness of the case of *Adams v. Lindsell*.

Accordingly, rather than it being the case that the views of Bell and Stair were thrown out by the positive law of Scotland, however, it would seem that it is the view of the Court of Session as expressed in *Countess of Dunmore* that stands as the anomaly. Indeed, following the House of Lords case of *Dunlop v. Higgins*,[76] the views of Bell, and so Stair, can be taken to stand as fundamentally representative of the principles underpinning the formation of voluntary obligations in Scotland. With that said, however, it has been said by MacQueen that the 1855 Inner House case of *Thomson v. James*[77] – not the earlier case of *Countess of Dunmore* – which 'proved [to be] the decisive step away from [the underlying principles of Stair and Bell], in effect re-modelling the rules of offer and acceptance'.[78] If this view is accepted as reflective of the law post-*Thomson*, then the great irony would be that the departure from the principle-based, deductive jurisprudence characteristic of Scots law, coupled with the adoption of a fundamentally Common law conception of 'offer + acceptance = contract' would have been effected by the Supreme Courts of Scotland itself, rather than through the officious decreets of an Anglicising House of Lords. Accordingly, analysis of *Thomson v. James* – 'by a long way, our most important case on offer and acceptance'[79] – is necessary, as it is here submitted that the extent to which it in fact deviates from Stair and Bell may, in fact, be critically questioned.

Thomson v. James and Acceptance by Post

From the above, it appears fair to suggest that – whatever language may in fact have been adopted by the courts in the early nineteenth century – Scots law did not in fact recognise a nominate 'postal acceptance rule', nor did it receive any such thing from English law, nor in fact can the law of Scotland be said to be the same as the law of England, due to the clear differences in basic principle, doctrine and method that permeate the jurisdictions. Nonetheless, like England, Scots law recognised, by the mid-nineteenth century (as indeed long before this point, even in the absence of positive judicial decisions endorsing such),[80] that a positive act of engagement, amounting to an acceptance, would be sufficient to conclude a contract even in the absence of communication to the offeree. The distinction between Scots and English law is thus subtle, but extremely important: in English law, the rule appears exceptional, but in Scotland, insofar as it exists, it does so as a function of the system's general doctrine. This notwithstanding, since at least the time of *Thomson v. James*,[81] decided in 1855, it has been implicitly assumed that Scots and English law are entirely as one on this point, that is, there has long been a distinct 'perception that the postal rule [is] an exception to the general rule, not itself reflecting the norm'.[82]

Though the groundwork allowing for perceived perfect commonality between Scots and English law may have been laid by the Lord Chancellor in *Dunlop*, despite his appropriate consideration of Bell therein, it was not until the 1855 Court of Session decision in *Thomson* that Scots law really began, in the words of MacQueen, to adopt the 'the lines of thought on requirements of communication apparent in Lord Newton's opinion' in *Countess of Dunmore v. Alexander*.[83] 'Yet' in MacQueen's words, 'at the very moment it overturned Bell's approach and established communication as a general requirement, the court entrenched a exception for postal acceptances. While relying heavily on Stair's theory of contract, the Court moved away from any notion that contract was about the concurrent wills of the parties.'[84]

That a single decision of the Inner House could have such a profound effect – seemingly deviating from the positive authority of the House of Lords as expressed in *Dunlop v. Higgins*, as well as the philosophical and rational reasoning of two of Scotland's finest Institutional writers – is remarkable. This is particularly so given that the case seemingly had this effect in spite of 'the internal contradictions in each of the majority opinions'.[85] In the main, *per* Lubbe, 'although not wholly united in their reasoning, the majority in coming to [their] conclusion was influenced not only by Bell, but also by the judgment in *Higgins*'.[86] Being that both Bell and Lord Chancellor Cottenham (the only judge to opine in *Higgins*) can be said to each ultimately adhere to the view that, *per* Stair, contracts are formed by reciprocal acts of 'engagement', and that communication is not a necessary element of such, quite how it can be contended that *Thomson* radically altered the law falls to be critically questioned.[87]

The case, ultimately, concerned the question of revocation of an offer. 'The majority of the court agreed [with the ruling of Lord President McNeill] that an attempted revocation of the offer which had not reached the offeree before posting was ineffective, even though it might have been posted before acceptance'.[88] This, it is submitted, seems self-contradictory if the views of Stair are adhered to, and 'offer' and 'acceptance' alike properly identified as species of 'engagement'. Just as an act of engagement intention to create a binding unilateral promise does not require communication for the obligation to come into being, and so from this it can be inferred that an acceptance does not require communication to bring into being a binding bilateral contract either, so too is it logically the case that communication of the withdrawal of an offer is not required to effectively 'kill' it off and obviate the possibility of its effective acceptance.[89] Hence, if an act of engagement amounting to 'acceptance' occurs before an act of engagement amounting to withdrawal of an offer, then logically the contract must be taken to be concluded and the parties thereto bound. Conversely, if the act of engagement which purports to withdraw the offer is effected before the offeree engages so as to accept it, no contract can be formed as the offeror has, through their will, made manifest their desire not to engage (i.e. to revoke the 'power of exaction' vested in the offeree). Absent some issue arising from the doctrine of personal bar, or the presence of some accessory obligation (such as that arising from a unilateral promise) to keep an offer open for a certain time, the offeree bears the risk that the offeror might withdraw, just as the offeror bears the risk that the offeree might accept and so bind the parties to a mutual obligation.

This view was not adopted by any of the judges in *Thomson*.[90] Notwithstanding this, Lubbe observed that 'the judgments in *Thomson v James* are marked by attempts to justify the positions adopted by reference to the views of Stair'.[91] Lord Curriehill, for his part, in a 'powerful dissent',[92] criticised Bell for providing 'no authority in support of [his] remark'[93] concerning postal acceptance. Though Lord Curriehill notes that Bell's observation 'is correct enough as to several classes of cases, such, for example, as those in which there is an unconditional promise [...] it is not consistent with the principles of the law of Scotland relative to the completion of onerous [by which Lord Curriehill can be taken to mean "mutual" or δ ι π λ ε υ ρ ο ς] contracts'.[94] Notwithstanding his criticism of Bell, Lord Curriehill did critically consider Stair's typology of 'acts of the will', although ultimately he formed the view that 'the pursuer's letter of acceptance, so long as it was undelivered and unknown to the defender, was ineffectual to bind them'.[95] This was so on the basis of the fact that, in his view, 'until the acceptance reached the offeree, there was not that *conventio in idem placitum* which is necessary to constitute a mutual contract. Until then, the pursuers had not conferred upon the defender that power of exacting performance of the counterpart of the offer [...] their consent was merely a resolution, with no such effect.'[96]

Lord Deas' decision – which, unlike Lord Curriehill's, accorded with the majority's view as to what the outcome of the case should be, if not perfectly with the reasoning of his brothers on the Bench – by contrast maintained that 'the power of exaction was conferred merely by the act of acceptance, pointing out that Stair made no mention of "any farther act, mental or physical, after the appropriate act of the acceptor, necessary to the completion of the contract"'.[97] This, it is submitted, is the correct view of Stair's account of 'engagement' (though his Lordship erred in holding that the posting of a retraction 'which neither did nor could' reach the recipient was in all cases ineffectual).[98] While Lord Curriehill took the view that an offeree who posted an acceptance 'might have recalled it before it arrived at its destination, and have still destroyed it. Or after so despatching it he might have sent an express with a refusal of the offer, and if it had been first delivered, he would still have been free, and the treaty would have been at an end',[99] this view appears not only self-contradictory, but fundamentally at odds with the view that voluntary obligations are formed by 'acts of the will'.

One cannot lose sight of the fact that, for Stair, reasoning as he was from general principle, the legal position was that promises, offers and acceptances were as one – species, or examples, of 'engagement' rather than free-floating and quintessentially several concepts. As such, if it suffices – as it did for Stair and does in modern Scots law – to say that a promise to bind the promisor without communication, then logically it follows that the acceptor of an offer likewise mutually binds the parties at the moment of acceptance. Likewise, though none of the judges in *Thomson* considered this possibility, the corollary of the fact that a promise and acceptance can effectively create an obligation must logically be that the withdrawal of an offer without communication is likewise efficacious to obviate the possibility of acceptance.

'Promise' is not a special case sequestrated from the law of 'contract'; 'promise' and 'contract' alike are both simply modes by which enforceable personal rights come into being. Hence, when Lord Curriehill recognised that Bell's view concerning communication conforms to the requirements for the creation of promise, it should logically have followed from this that the principle was applicable *mutatis mutandis* to offers and acceptances alike. That this was not recognised by Lord Curriehill (nor for that matter the other judges) may have been a result of the peculiar rules of form which existed in Scots law until the passing of the Requirements of Writing (Scotland) Act 1995; indeed, his Lordship does speak, at some length, about the significance of delivery to the execution of missives (i.e. contracts concerned with the conveyance of heritable property) in his judgement.[100] It may also have been due to influence from the Civil law and its ossified, events-based approach to the categorisation of 'contracts': indeed, it is perhaps of some relevance that Lord Curriehill remarked that '[his] confidence in the general principle, stated by Lord Newton as the ground of the judgment in the case of Lady Dunmore, is much strengthened by the circumstance that that eminent judge was for a considerable time Professor of Civil law in the University of Edinburgh'.[101]

With its principally events-based classification of 'contract law', the intellectual approach of the Civil law proper can be said to be most unlike that which Stair utilised. Indeed, this approach is, as Birks observed, altogether more like that similar events-based taxonomy present, though generally unarticulated, in English law.[102] The Scottish tradition – as articulated and influenced by Stair – is and was distinct from the approach utilised by the two 'great legal families'; although, of course, the small jurisdiction has never been able to escape the influence of twin titans. 'The rather peripheral attention given to Stair's view in *Thomson v James* should not [then] be taken as meaning that his influence was unimportant [...] the subject [of offer and acceptance] is not central to Stair's treatment'.[103] Stair's account was, as has been explained, concerned with the 'bigger picture' of Scots law, as a system, while the considerations of the Bench in *Thomson v. James* were naturally far narrower and concerned principally with the question of 'formation of contract', rather than 'formation of voluntary obligations'. Hence, fundamentally, it cannot be so much said that *Thomson v. James* changed the law of Scotland (indeed, the altogether more recent case of *Park, Petitioner* is readily capable of being analysed with reference to Stair's taxonomy of 'engagement'),[104] but it should be noted that the case may be said to mark something of a turning point for the Scots legal system, by which 'the Scottish predilection for reasoning on general principle [was abandoned] in favour of a more casuistic approach, exemplified by the focus on the postal contract as a special case'.[105] This casuistic approach may well have been justified as somewhat necessary against the backdrop of complex rules of procedure and evidence extant at the time of the decision, but it is here submitted that this methodology is not suitable in modern Scots law. The complex rules of evidence that plagued the courts of the nineteenth and twentieth centuries have been swept away by the Requirements of Writing (Scotland) Act 1995. Again, Scots legal academics – as well as those with the luxury of time for research and reflection, as well as the ear of (at least one of Scotland's two) Parliament(s),[106] such as the Scottish Law Commissioners[107] – must lead the charge in developing a jurisprudence, and so law and legal system, founded on reason rather than merely on the positive authority of some political decision(s).

Towards Abolition of the 'Postal Rule'?

In 1993, the Scottish Law Commission came to recommend the abolishment of the so-called 'postal acceptance rule', on the basis that it 'gives rise to well recognised difficulties'.[108] The difficulties identified in the Commission's report are each answerable by reference to the general principles pertaining to the formation of voluntary obligations as espoused by Stair and, later, Bell. The Commission asked 'what happens, for example, if the letter of acceptance is lost in the post and never arrives?', inferring that 'logically a contract has been concluded, but some Scottish judges have doubted whether this would actually be held to be the law if the situation arose [as per Lord Shand in *Mason v Benhar Coal Co.*]'.[109] It is here submitted that the logic that a contract has in fact been concluded is unimpeachable on the basis of principle, being that the act of posting an acceptance clearly amounts to 'engagement' in the sense espoused by Stair.[110] By posting the letter of acceptance, the offeree plainly demonstrates, objectively, their will to be bound, conferring a power of exaction in the offeror and showing themselves committed to perform their part of the bargain.

As was indicated earlier, Lord President Hamilton observed in the 2007 case of *Cawdor v. Cawdor*, 'the presence or absence of communication to the other party may be an adminicle of evidence in the question whether the statement amounts to a promise in law'[111] and this statement can – being that promises and acceptances are each species of effectual engagement – be applied *mutatis mutandis* to 'acceptances' as well as 'promises'. In essence, then, a party who seeks to claim that they did in fact post an acceptance may face evidentiary difficulties in satisfying a court, on the balance of probabilities, that they did in fact engage so as to create a contract as they will necessarily be lacking a significant piece of evidence that the letter was in fact posted. The difficulty, though, is purely evidentiary; it is not an issue of substantive law. If it be juridically proven that the letter was in fact posted, then even if it was never ultimately delivered, the offeree – having been proven to have engaged in such a fashion as to conclude the agreement – is bound, along with the offeror, *ex contractu* to perform their respective undertakings.

The Commission went on to query 'what if the acceptance is withdrawn by telegram, telex, fax or telephone after it had been posted but before it had reached the offeror?', again noting that 'logically, the withdrawal is too late, because a contract has already been concluded, but this result may seem unpalatable'. Quite why the result should be thought unpalatable is difficult to conceive, however – although certainly there are those who take the view that 'from a policy perspective [...] the postal rule has fallen largely out of favour'.[112] It might equally be said that the innocent offeree – who does everything that they can do to signify their engagement – who is frustrated in their endeavours to communicate the acceptance by faulty service provision should not bear the disappointment of their expectation that a contract has been concluded by their endeavours. One who makes a written offer, inviting response by post, necessarily leaves open the possibility of the offeree acting in reliance on that offer and indeed ultimately engaging so as to accept that offer. In essence, by engaging with the offeree by conferring upon them the power to conclude an agreement, the offeror can be taken to have knowingly committed themselves to the prospect of being contractually bound. That they may become such without the fact having been communicated to them seems immaterial, given that they have – as a matter of law – shown themselves committed to the course; this of course combines with the fact that, in recognising 'promise', 'offer' and 'acceptance' as species of engagement, communication ought not to be required to effectively withdraw an offer.

The other 'difficulties' raised by the Commission can likewise be disposed of by reference to basic principles of legal logic. They ask 'what if the letter is wrongly addressed, or unstamped?', noting that 'there is no Scottish authority directly in point'. In the absence of such, the answer is plain: the outcome will depend on whether or not the party who sent the incorrectly addressed or unstamped letter seriously intended to 'conferreth or stateth a power of exaction in' the offeror. This is not a question that can – or should – be answered in the abstract; it will necessarily depend on the facts and circumstances of the particular case in question. The law must know the full facts surrounding the 'event' in question to determine an appropriate response; it is intellectually (and so becomes practically) unsatisfactory to legislate a general rule for the particular. Other questions raised – particularly those in connection with the place of 'qualified acceptances' in this schema – can likewise be disposed of with reference to general principle; in terms of 'fundamental structural language' there is in fact no such concept as a 'qualified acceptance' since such invariably amounts to a fresh offer,[113] killing the original offer in turn.[114] Far from it being 'anomalous to have one rule for unqualified acceptances and another for qualified acceptances', it is in fact in inescapable consequence of the fact that so-called 'qualified acceptances' are not in fact acceptances, but rather counter-offers, with all of the consequences that entails.

Accordingly, many of the questions asked by the Scottish Law Commission – in particular the following: 'How far does the rule apply to quasi-postal acceptances? Does it apply if the letter is passed to a letter exchange scheme or to a private messenger? Does it apply to telegrams? Does it apply to acceptances by telex? What if a telex communication is not instantaneous – because the message is sent out of hours? What about an acceptance sent by fax? If the rule does apply to an acceptance by fax, what if the acceptance is fed into the sender's fax machine but, because of a fault in the recipient's machine, emerges in an unreadable form? What about various forms of electronic data interchange?' – can be said to be asked from the starting point of a false premise. If the 'postal acceptance rule' is not conceived of as an exceptional case, but as an illustration of the general principles of contract formation in this jurisdiction, then each of the above can be answered with reference to Stair's schema. Ultimately, the question ought to remain – does the offeree's conduct amount to a reciprocal act of 'engagement'? If the answer is yes, then a contract can be taken to have been concluded at that moment of engagement. If the answer is no, then it has not. Again, this cannot really be answered in the abstract, since the particular facts of each particular case will need to be considered, but application of the principles espoused by Stair to those particular cases should in the end provide logical answers.

One final point, raised by the SLC's report of 2018, merits direct address: at para.4.92, the Commission suggests that 'the speed with which written and oral communications may be made through modern technology' essentially 'suggests that there is also no real need to protect the offeree in the competition between revocation and acceptance'[115] and that, by logical extension, the onus for ensuring the effective communication of acceptance should be firmly placed upon the offeree. This, however, seems to put an unwarranted amount of faith in the infallibility of modern means of communication. Just as letters could go missing in the Victorian age (if only most 'extraordinarily', given the otherwise excellent Victorian postal service),[116] so too is it the case now that an email, text message or other such missive may fail to deliver not through fault of the sender, but due to a neglectful service provider. Presently, given the principles laid down by Stair and Bell, and accepted by judicial figures across the Scottish courts, it would appear that one able to juridically prove that a message was in fact sent, even if not received, would be able to found upon the existence of a contract. The proposals of the SLC would reverse this position, to the detriment of persons frustrated in their attempts to conclude agreements by the vagaries of external phenomena such as bad service, bad weather or any number of other potential disruptive occurrences. It was said, in the report, that scenarios in which 'the offeree neither knows nor has reason to know that there has been delay' in delivery of the acceptance 'are not common in legal practice'.[117] Whether or not such delays are common, or otherwise, is immaterial, however. The law, by necessity, must be capable of adapting to, and accounting for, the uncommon and unexpected. Consequently, in the absence of more detailed consideration of the significant changes that would be effected by turning the law of Scotland, concerned with the formation of voluntary obligations, on its head, it is thought that the legislature should leave well enough alone.

Conclusion

Scots private law has the benefit of a rational and ordered 'intellectual superstructure' which allows anyone possessed of reason to deduce the principles applicable to given cases and determine the applicable law as a result.[118] This philosophical achievement should not be thrown away for the mere temporal expedience of alignment with a geographical and politically connected, but juridically quite distinct, neighbour, nor should it be sacrificed at the altar of piecemeal codification. There is, after all, a reason that Parliament was, in the mid-1960s, initially reluctant to expand the remit of the Law Commissions Act 1965 to apply to Scotland.[119] Wilson-Stark takes the view that it is a 'fair assessment' to say that '"English circumstances and English pressures" led to the 1965 Act, with the provisions for Scotland "tacked" on';[120] indeed, it is in fact notable that 'Scots law was believed to be in less need of reform than English law, due to its Civilian heritage and restatement of the civil law by Stair in the Seventeenth Century'.[121]

While, then, there were some in Parliament who would preach 'legitimate pride in the superiority of English law over Roman law and other foreign systems',[122] it was then recognised even by such figures that this attitude has 'often blinded [English lawyers] to the experience that can sometimes be derived from developments in the Commonwealth and other countries, to say nothing of Scotland'.[123] Stair's inheritance – preached as so enduring and vital, particularly in respect of the law pertaining to voluntary obligations – is one which can and ought to be made use of in preference to fractured and disjointed legislative reform. Rather than presenting a taxonomy that is 'stuck in the Seventeenth Century',[124] Stair produced an *opus* that is 'so well digested in all its parts, so liberal in principle, so good in arrangement, so distinguished for sound judgment and excellent adaptation to the business and concerns of men that it would seem almost beyond the age in which it was written'.[125] Teachers, scholars and even prospective reformers of Scots law ought, consequently, to pay due regard to Stair's intellectual efforts in order to ascertain what the law is and ought to be according to first principles, with a view to rationalising and explaining the operation of the law as it stands.

The prerogative of the Scottish Law Commissioner is not at all, however, the same as the prerogative of the Scottish law professor (or, for that matter, scholar or teacher of lesser – or no – academic rank). A Law Commission, in its modern sense, by its nature, 'is not single-purpose, but multi-purpose, not time-limited but open-ended, at least in intention'.[126] Under the establishing legislation, it is 'the duty of each of the Commissioners to take and keep under review all the law with which they are respectively concerned with a view to its systematic development and reform, in particular the codification of such law, elimination of anomalies, the repeal of obsolete and unnecessary enactments, the reduction of the number of separate enactments, and generally the simplification and modernisation of the law'.[127] It is this impetus to 'codification', as well as 'modernisation', that marks a major distinction between the Commissioner and the Teacher; while these two *personae* may be united in desire to eliminate anomalies from the law, see a reduction in the number of separate enactments and see the law largely simplified, the Law Commissioner, in their drive for reform, codification and 'modernisation', may be content with the introduction of 'quasi-codifying statutes in particular area[s] [...] [which] at least have the merit of stating authoritatively what the law is, for good or ill'.[128] The 'relatively time-rich professor' – engaged as they are in the study and teaching of *ius* (by which it is here meant the law that can be deduced and rationalised by exercise of right reason)[129] and free of the burden to advocate for legislation – ought not to advocate introduction of and thereafter submission to the strictures of some *lex* regardless of its merits. With the statutory duty to advocate for the codification and 'modernisation' of law, however, the Commissioners are almost by necessity bound to support legislative reform of the law. This, as the next chapter shall explore in detail, places Law Commissioners, and the SLC, in something of a 'double-bind' given the fact that they stand simultaneously bound to discharge duties which militate against the proliferation of (particularly, piecemeal) statutory enactments.

Notes

1 *Chitty on Contracts*, para.4.065.

2 *Brinkibon Ltd v. Stahag Stahl etc.* [1983] 2 A.C. 34.

3 The proposition that an offer is not deemed to be accepted until the acceptance is communicated to the offeror has long-standing pedigree in English case law: See *McIver v. Richardson* (1813) 1 M. & S. 557; *Mozley v. Tinkler* (1835) 1 C.M. & R. 692; *Ex p. Stark* [1897] 1 Ch. 575; *Holwell Securities Ltd v. Hughes* [1974] 1 W.L.R. 155, 157; *Allied Marine Transport Ltd v. Vale do Rio Doce Navegaçao SA (The Leonidas D.)* [1985] 1 W.L.R. 925, 937; *Air Transworld Ltd v. Bombardier Inc* [2012] EWHC 243 (Comm), [2012] 1 Lloyd's Rep 349.

4 *Adams v. Lindsell* (1818) 1 B & Ald 681; 106 E.R 250

5 Though cf. Nick Sage, *The Significance of Adams v. Lindsell*, [2020] JCL 179.

6 *Chitty on Contracts*, para.1.050.

7 As Blackie observed in 1974 however, it has in fact 'never been clear in Scotland [...] that there [is] a definite rule': the 'broad statement of principle', to the effect that 'acceptance by post, that is by posting a letter of acceptance, completes the contract': John W.G. Blackie, *Loss in the Post: Uncertainty of the Law*, [1974] JLSS 134, at 134; see also *Jacobsen Sons & Co v. Underwood & Sons Ltd.* (1894) 21 R 654 at 657. For a more recent decision which expresses the idea of a nominate 'postal acceptance rule', see *Carmarthen Developments Limited v. Samuel James Pennington* [2008] CSOH 139.

8 See, e.g., the opinion of Lord Deas in *Thomson v. James* (1855) 18 D. 1 at 26–27; see further to the opinion of Lord Young in *Jacobsen Sons & Co v. Underwood & Sons Ltd.* (1894) 21 R 654 at 657, who makes plain his view that cases of this kind are 'ruled by the principle stated by Professor Bell in the passage quoted by the Lord Ordinary' (i.e. Bell, *Commentaries*, at 326–327).

9 Sheridan, *Contract Law in Flux*.
10 See Bogle, *Contract*, 71.
11 See fn.5.
12 See fn.6.
13 *Jacobsen Sons & Co v. Underwood & Sons Ltd.* (1894) 21 R 654 at 657 *per* Lord Justice Clerk MacDonald, citing Bell, *Commentaries*, 326–327.
14 Contract (Formation) (Scotland) Bill, s.4.
15 (1894) 21 R. 654.
16 Ibid., at 655.
17 Cf. *Park, Petitioner* [2009] CSOH 122. Here, the court considered the prospective application of the principles concerning 'postal acceptance' to faxed communications, finding that 'at the moment of posting, the granter puts the writing beyond his control. The position with regard to a fax is different. The granter of the writing retains the custody of the writing but a copy of it is created electronically in the hands of the recipient [...] the question is whether the fact of the recipient having received that copy is sufficient to prevent the granter from being able to destroy it. Is the granter barred from doing so by the fact of the fax transmission, or has he done no more than demonstrate to the recipient of the fax the existence of the principal which is still in the hands of the granter? In my opinion the answer to that question depends upon the intention of the parties which may be derived either from a general practice [...] [or] from a specific agreement': at para.22–23. This view can be seen to be consistent with that expressed by Bell, who took the view that in the general course of business 'it is the act of acceptance that binds the bargain', but that 'to this [...] an exception may be made by the offerer, limiting it so that the arrival of the acceptance only shall bind the bargain': Bell, *Commentaries*, at 326–327. Applied *mutatis mutandis* to the case of acceptance by fax, it would appear to be that the baseline position is that the act of faxing marks the conclusion of the contract, unless the offerer has stipulated that delivery of the principal shall be necessary to 'bind the bargain', or there is proven to be an extant business practice of generally requiring such.
18 Shepherd & Wedderburn, 'Goodbye "Postal Acceptance Rule," Hello "Out-of-Office Message" Rule?' 5 September 2017, at https://goo.gl/5evhjK.
19 As they have consistently advocated for since the 1970s: para.4.89.
20 Watson, *Slave Law*, 36.
21 Para.2.1.
22 In Swaminathan's terminology: see Shivprasad Swaminathan, *The Will Theorist's Mailbox: Misunderstanding the Moment of Contract Formation in the Indian Contract Act 1872*, [2018] Statute Law Review 14, 15.
23 (1818) 1 B & Ald 681.
24 Robert J. Pothier, *Traité des Obligations* (Chez Rouzeau-Montaut, 1761), translated into English by François X. Martin, *A Treatise on Obligations: Considered in a Moral and Legal View* (Martin and Ogden, 1802).
25 Swaminathan, *The Will Theorist's Mailbox*, 14, 15.
26 Hogg, *Perspectives*, 648.
27 Ibid., 649–650.
28 Bell, *Commentaries*, ix.
29 Henry Cockburn, *Circuit Journeys* (David Douglas, 1888), 203.
30 Bell, *Commentaries*, 293.

31 In her 'case study in [Bell's] method', MacGregor notes that 'Bell cites Civilian sources throughout his treatment of partnership law. French law predominates, particularly Pothier's famous treatise on the law of partnership [*Traité du Contract de Société* (1775)]'. With that said, however, 'the comparative material is not [...] used as inspiration for the future direction of Scots law. Rather it appears to be provided for the interest of the reader [...] references to the work of Civilian authors are significantly outnumbered by references to case law': Laura MacGregor, 'Introduction' in George Joseph Bell, *Commentaries on the Laws of Scotland and on the Principles of Mercantile Jurisprudence*, Volume I (Edinburgh Legal Education Trust, 2023), xxii.

32 MacQueen, 'Distance Contracting', 47, 54.

33 MacGregor, 'Introduction', at xii.

34 Ibid., at xii, citing p.550 of Volume 1.

35 Bell, *Commentaries*, 293.

36 Indeed, *per* Lord President Glencorse, 'a contract which cannot be enforced by specific implement, in so far as regards its form and substance, is no contract at all' – *M'Arthur v. Lawson* (1877) 4 R. 1134, 1136.

37 Microsoft Word informs me that this is not a real word, but the Oxford English Dictionary suggests otherwise, stating that the word has been in continuous – if infrequent – use in print since 1664. This was, apparently, a good year for beer according to Kronenbourg's 2005 advert, https://www.youtube.com/watch?v=8xLykuM0Vrs.

38 See *Retail Parks Investments Ltd v. The Royal Bank of Scotland Plc (No 2)* 1996 S.C. 227 at 244 *per* Lord Cullen, noting the differences between Scots and English law in this regard.

39 For Bell, '[obediential] obligations are sometimes as perfect as a conventional obligation; sometimes imperfect, not requiring the interference of a court of justice, but more conventionally left to the jurisdiction and enforcements of conscience alone'. Bell, *Commentaries*, at 293–294. It is thought that this view would have been – if not entirely inconceivable – vehemently rejected by Stair as anathema. It is here submitted that Bell's view is justifiable only because his focus in the *Commentaries* is on mercantile jurisprudence (and so principally on conventional obligations); unlike Stair, he is not concerned with the taxonomy of the whole of Scots law (at least, the whole of the law cognisable before the Court of Session at Stair's time of writing), nor on delict nor reparation for wrongdoing generally.

40 Bell, *Commentaries*, 293.

41 It is notable, in fact, that Bell continuously seeks to rationalise obligations which arise *ex lege* as – essentially – quasi-contractual (going so far as to suggest that conventional and obediential obligations may otherwise be called those 'express' and those 'implied' – at 293). Indeed, in his (extremely limited) discussion of *negotiorum gestio*, Bell considers this legal institution – which (*inter alia*) imposes an *ex lege* obligation on one party to reimburse the expenses of the other – to be a 'contract' despite the fact that it arises from neither agreement nor consensus nor consent (this peculiarity being, in fact, a fundamental hallmark of the concept): Bell, *Commentaries*, 269.

42 Ibid., 294.

43 Ibid., 334–431.

44 MacQueen and Thomson, for instance, define a 'contract' as 'an agreement between two or more persons (the parties) having capacity to make it, in the form demanded

by law, to perform, on one side or both, acts which are not trifling, indeterminate, impossible or illegal' (*MacQueen and Thomson*, para.1.10). This is a fine definition, but for the fact that it can be criticised as misleading, giving the impression that the latter half of it applies only to contracts, when in fact (with the tactical omission of 'on one side or both') the requirements listed in the second half of the definition can in fact be applied with minimal adaptation to the constitution of any unilateral obligation, testament or trust. That is to say, one can effectively reframe the second half of the obligation to hold that any act of the will, to bring about legal consequence (i.e. to create a binding *ex voluntate* obligation, trust or testament) must adhere to set formal requirements, be effected by one with requisite capacity and cannot concern matters trifling, indeterminate, impossible or illegal. It is too narrow to identify these features as incidents of 'contracts' only.

45 Ibid., 334.

46 Ibid., 326.

47 Ibid.

48 MacQueen, 'Distance Contracting', 55.

49 (1818) 1 B & Ald 681.

50 See the opinion of the Lord Chancellor in *Dunlop v. Higgins* (1848) 1 HLC 381, at 400, though note that his Lordship's declaration that 'the law of Scotland appears to be the same as the law of England' must, as in all cases in which a declaration of this kind is made, be taken with a large pinch of salt. The same outcome, on the facts of *Dunlop*, may be reached in Scotland and England alike, but that in no way implies parity of general jurisprudence or legal principle.

51 Bogle, *Contract*, 71.

52 MacGregor, 'Introduction', vi.

53 Bell, *Commentaries*, 326–327.

54 Ibid., at 327.

55 MacQueen, 'Distance Contracting', 56.

56 (1830) 9 S 190.

57 T.B. Smith, *Short Commentary on the Law of Scotland* (W. Green, 1962), 764.

58 (1830) 9 S 190, 191.

59 Ibid., 194.

60 MacQueen, 'Distance Contracting', 57.

61 Ibid. This view was not, obviously, taken to reflect the law of Scotland in subsequent case law, given that it is well settled that a promise may be constituted by communication to an unrelated third party: *Cawdor v. Cawdor* 2007 SC 285, para.15.

62 Ibid., 58.

63 As MacQueen notes, 'the doctrine of offer and acceptance emerges fully fledged as part of the general law of contract in the 1860 edition' of Erskine's *Principles* (edited by J. Guthrie Smith) having appeared only in relation to contracts by word and writ in previous editions: MacQueen, 'Distance Contracting', fn.81. Consider, also, e.g., Gloag's view that 'an offer requires acceptance, communicated in some way to the offeror' Gloag, *Contract*, 26.

64 Indeed, if it were – it might be suggested – the SLC would not need to advocate for the enactment of legislation to put the matter beyond doubt and enshrine the need for communication in law.

65 In *Dunlop v. Higgins* (1847) 9 D. 1413.

66 In *Dunlop*, his Lordship expressed the view that he could 'not see how there can be an *in idem pactum concursus et convention* [*sic*] between two parties when one of them remains in entire ignorance of the fact [of acceptance]' – (1847) 9 D. 1413, at 1422.
67 *Dunlop v. Higgins* (1848) 1 HLC 381.
68 Ibid., 400.
69 (1841) 7 Mee and Wels 515.
70 (1818) 1 B & Ald 681.
71 Phillip H. Brodie (Lord Brodie), 'From Scotland and Ireland' in Louis Blom-Cooper, Brice Dickson and Gavin Drewry (eds), *The Judicial House of Lords 1876–2009* (Oxford University Press, 2009), 289.
72 Such 'legal imperialism', high-handedly 'imposing unwelcome and retrograde English doctrine' upon Scots law, was not of course wholly absent from the nineteenth-century House of Lords – as the infamous case of *Bartonshill Coal Co. v. Reid* (1858) 3 Macq 266 manifestly demonstrates. Yet as Lord Brodie points out, even in such egregious cases 'the groundwork [was] put in by [...] Scots lawyers': Brodie, 'From Scotland and Ireland', at 292.
73 *Dunlop v. Higgins* (1848) 1 HLC 381, 400.
74 Indeed, his Lordship noted that the conclusions of the English courts were consistent with Bell's view and that 'nothing has been stated to us in contradiction of his opinion', thus implying that had such contradictory material been cited to the court then the judgement would have been quite different (see *Dunlop*, at 400). Note, here, that *Countess of Dunmore* was in fact cited before the court, but that the citation of this case did not ultimately persuade the House of Lords to depart from the views found in Bell and so Stair.
75 Bell, *Commentaries*, 293–294.
76 (1848) 1 HLC 381.
77 (1855) 18 D. 1.
78 MacQueen, 'Distance Contracting', 60.
79 McBryde, *Contract*, para.6–12.
80 That is not to say that such judicial decisions were in fact absent – merely that even if they were, due to the deductive, reason-and-principle-based approach of Scots law, the absence of positive authority affirming a view is not fatal to a claim as to the veracity of that view.
81 (1855) 18 D. 1.
82 MacQueen, 'Distance Contracting', 68.
83 Ibid., 60.
84 Ibid.
85 Ibid.
86 Lubbe, 'Formation of Contract', 37.
87 As MacQueen himself notes, 'Bell's statement of the law remained unaltered in the seventh and final edition of the *Commentaries* (published 1870)': MacQueen, 'Distance Contracting', at 67.
88 Lubbe, 'Formation of Contract', 36.
89 Such is recognised as logically sound by Lord Curriehill in his dissenting judgement in *Thomson*: *Thomson v. James* (1855) 18 D. 1, 20.
90 Lord Ivory's opinion comes close, but does not articulate this in exactly these terms: see *Thomson v. James* (1855) 18 D. 1, 14–16.
91 Lubbe, 'Formation of Contract', 37.

92 Ibid.
93 *Thomson v. James* (1855) 18 D. 1, 22.
94 Ibid.
95 Ibid., 20.
96 Ibid., 19.
97 Ibid., 26; Lubbe, 'Formation of Contract', 38.
98 *Thomson v. James* (1855) 18 D. 1, at 24. Logically, if the retraction were proven to have been posted before the acceptance, then there would be no offer open to accept. From the facts as articulated in the report of *Thomson*, however, it is unclear if the retraction was posted before, or after, the acceptance: the acceptance was posted at some time 'between half past two and half past four on the 1st December 1853' while the revocation was posted 'before 3pm', though no precise time could be identified. Given that the precise timing was unknown (in the absence of further evidence) if not unknowable, the difficulties with applying the principles espoused by Stair are manifest. That is not, however, sufficient reason to justify departing from those principles; rather, it ought to have served merely as impetus to gather further evidence about the precise time of the twin postings.
99 *Thomson v James* (1855) 18 D. 1, at 20.
100 Ibid., 20.
101 Ibid., 23.
102 Birks, 'Definition and Division', 35.
103 Lubbe, 'Formation of Contract', 38.
104 [2009] CSOH 122, particularly at para.23. It may be suggested here that 'engagement' is taken to be 'the moment [...] the granter puts the writing beyond his control'.
105 Ibid.
106 Though the Scottish civil service – and by associated government and wider Parliament – 'has never been hostile to the SLC', the same cannot be said of Westminster. 'Whitehall has never liked the commissions. That was true in the beginning and it remains true': Gretton, *Law Commissioning*, 149.
107 For an insight into the work of Scottish Law Commissioners, see Gretton, *Law Commissioning*, 135–144.
108 Scottish Law Commission, *Report on Formation of Contract: Scottish Law and the United Nations Convention on Contracts for the International Sale of Goods*, (14 June 1993) Scot. Law Com. 144, para.4.4.
109 (1882) 19 SLR 642.
110 In terms of positive authority, too, *Jacobsen Sons & Co v. Underwood & Sons Ltd.* (1894) 21 R 654 was decided some years after Lord Shand expressed his doubts and in that case the Inner House remained of the view that Bell's opinion as then continued to stand as the law of Scotland.
111 2007 SC 285, para.15.
112 Martin Hogg, *Contract Formation in the Electronic Age*, [2009] Edin. L. R. 121, 125.
113 *Howgate Shopping Centre Ltd. v. GLS 164 Ltd.* 2002 SLT 820.
114 *Wolf and Wolf v. Forfar Potato Co.* 1984 SLT 100.
115 SLC, *Report*, para.4.92.
116 See Blackie, *Loss in the Post* 134, assessing Lord President M'Neill's expression of shock that the notion that a letter might go missing in the case of *Thomson v. James* (1855) 18 D. 1, 11.

117 SLC, *Report*, para.5.36–5.37.

118 This, it might be argued, marks the 'democratic' aspect of Scotland's tradition of the 'democratic intellect': Of which, see George E. Davie, *The Democratic Intellect: Scotland and Her Universities in the Nineteenth Century* (Edinburgh University Press, 1961); George E. Davie, *The Crisis of the Democratic Intellect* (Polygon, 1986); D. Neil MacCormick, *The Democratic Intellect and the Law*, [1984] Legal Studies 172.

119 Shona Wilson-Stark, *The Longer You Can Look Back, The Further You CanLook Forward: The Origins of the Scottish Law Commission*, [2014] Edin. L.R. 59, 65.

120 Wilson-Stark, *Origins*, 65.

121 Ibid.

122 HC Debate 8 February 1965 col 55.

123 Ibid.

124 This aphorism was the redoubt of reformers who sought to 'modernise' the law pertaining to *ius quaesitum tertio*: See Mathie, *Third Party Rights – Scots Law Stuck in the 17th Century*.

125 Bell, *Commentaries*, ix.

126 Gretton, *Law Commissioning*, 121.

127 Law Commissions Act 1965, s.1 (3).

128 MacQueen, *Invincible*, 10.

129 Ulpian, at the outset of Justinian's Digest, tells us that *iuri operam daturum prius nosse oportet, unde nomen iuris descendat. est autem a iustitia appellatum: nam, ut eleganter Celsus definit, ius est ars boni et aequi*. 'One who wishes to learn and work with the law must necessarily first know whence the name *ius* descends. It is called such because it comes from *iustitia*, which is moreover defined elegantly by Celsus: *ius* is the art of goodness and fairness'. As Watson observes in his own translation of D.1.1.1, the word '*ius* cannot be exactly translated from Latin into English': Alan Watson, *The Digest of Justinian*, Volume 1 (University of Pennsylvania Press, 1985), at 1. Here, in line with the exposition of Stein's *Regulae Iuris*, *ius* is taken to mean the law as deduced from reason, as contrasted with *lex* which denotes law imposed by declaration of one with requisite authority.

Chapter 3

THE LAW COMMISSIONERS' DOUBLE-BIND

Introduction

It is notable that Law Commissions – at any rate 'multi-purpose, and not time-limited but open ended' Commissions – are essentially an institution of the Anglophone (though not exclusively Common law)[1] world.[2] Most jurisdictions do not have them and there is no doubt that they are not necessary entities – but the question of so-called 'necessity' is essentially distinct from that of beneficence, utility and so desirability.[3] It seems fair to say, as Gretton (himself a former Scottish Law Commissioner) did, that the Law Commissions have generally been thought desirable, within the United Kingdom at least, because 'although governments can do legal housekeeping, usually they don't, or do it in a cursory and slovenly manner'.[4] So-called 'legal housekeeping' can be taken to mean the sort of 'technical law reform' which is of greatest interest to lawyers (who wish to see the collective system of justice functioning well and may find fascination with matters which would bore the typical layperson)[5] albeit that it ultimately exists for the benefit of all in society.[6] While anything can be made 'political' by agitators, activists, pressure groups and the like,[7] the Commissions tend to (but do not always) steer clear of overtly 'political' matters.[8] The general 'rule of thumb' for the sort of law reform projects that are undertaken by the SLC is that 'the more likely an initiative is to be reported on the front pages [of general media sources] the less likely it is to be a commission initiative'.[9] Against this background, the SLC's move to reform 'contract law' seems unremarkable.

The perceived utility of establishing and maintaining some body dedicated to the task of law reform, particularly 'technical law reform' of this kind, would appear to correlate with the consequences arising from a phenomenon articulated in the 'general thesis' advanced by Alan Watson in his barnstorming study of *Slave Law in the Americas*.[10] That is, 'the lesson of history is that over most of the field of law and especially of private law, in most political and economic circumstances, rulers need have no interest in determining what the rules of law are or should be, provided always, of course, that revenues roll in and the public peace is kept. Rulers and their immediate underlings can be, and often have been and are, indifferent to the nature of legal rules in operation.'[11] Due to this indifference to the content of – particularly – private law rules, there exists an impetus for interested individuals – with technical, forensic expertise – to ensure that the development and operation of the law keeps pace with the evolving needs of society.[12] At various points in history, and across various legal traditions, this need has been filled with different classes of individuals, with greater or lesser proximity to some identifiable 'superior' or 'sovereign' whose 'jurisdiction and power' sanctions the process of creating, varying or affirming the law.[13] As is discussed in this chapter, the Scottish Law Commissioners can – subject to some significant qualifications – be located within this 'heroic' tradition of jurisprudents who effect rational legal change and shape the culture of their given legal system and tradition.[14]

There is no question that the SLC is comprised of eminently qualified individuals, comparatively time-rich[15] and dedicated to the task of bringing clarity to the law through 'technical' law reform of the kind that in centuries past has been brought about by jurists (i.e. 'technical' experts in law) rather than politicians or legislators. Yet these factors notwithstanding, there is a clear and inescapable distinction to be drawn between the commissioners and the jurists of centuries past. It is this: while 'the opinions of individual jurists or professors [and to this can even be added individual judges in the Common law tradition, prior to the entrenchment of a rigid doctrine of *stare decisis*][16] have to win general acceptance before they become legal rules',[17] with this 'acceptance' here stemming from fellow jurists rather than political society, the opinions of the SLC can be – and indeed, following the Scottish government's programme for the 2021–2026 Parliament, and presumably subsequent Parliaments are in fact likely to be – declared 'law' (*lex*) by fiat of the legislature.[18] The Scottish Parliament, being a legislature of devolved competence, has proven keen to exercise its faculty to produce new legislation – though its limited concern with the actual content of such legislation correlates with the observations made by Watson in respect of 'enthusiastic' and 'energetic' legislators such as Justinian, Napoleon and Atatürk.[19] That is to say, even where rulers (and Parliaments, as sovereign or superior decision-makers, fit a broad definition of the term 'rulers') who are concerned with improving the 'accessibility' of the law emerge, the actual content of the promulgated rules tends to be of 'generally less concern' than broad 'conform[ity] to a particular political or social ideal'.[20]

Scotland, presently, has a legislative body and executive that is keen to make its mark on the legal framework by legislating in and across those areas over which it possesses legal authority. It has, following recommendations of the SLC, passed legislation significantly reforming areas of private law as varied as defamation,[21] moveable transactions,[22] judicial factors,[23] trusts and succession.[24] In the course of making these reforms, Parliamentarians have shown a lack of concern for the precise content of the rules in these areas, as evidenced (*inter alia*)[25] by the fact that in the first instance they have largely outsourced their responsibility for the construction of legislation to the SLC. The SLC has, since the foundation of the devolved Parliament, reliably promoted the passing of legislation in each area of Scots law which they have reported on as a part of their programmes of law reform, almost always including some draft bill as a part of their final reports.[26] Although in 2025 a report which advocated the repeal of existing legislation, without replacement, rather than the introduction of some new Act was in fact published,[27] this was the first report, produced solely by the SLC,[28] since 2001 which did not include a draft bill for proposed enactment.[29] While, on the face of it, it would appear desirable for politicians to defer to expert opinion where matters of technical law reform are concerned, to assume such is to fail to appreciate that some – indeed, perhaps a great many – aspects of law are, within a largely uncodified system, best left untouched by legislation.[30] Yet, by the nature of the law commissioners' statutory duties – particularly their obligation to pay heed to the prospective 'codification' and 'modernisation' of the law – means that there exists a notable impetus for them to propose legislative intervention in all cases. Combining this perceived impetus with the fact of a Parliament which has proven keen to enact the recommendations of the SLC, the temptation to propose some new enactment in any given area under review is manifest. Being comprised, as all organisations ultimately are, of human beings, the SLC, alas, may now be as keen to revel in the 'éclat of a new extension' as are those politicians criticised, by Gretton, for this propensity.[31]

In recognition of this, the present chapter seeks to examine the extent to which the Scottish law commissioners are presently caught in a 'double-bind' as a result of their wide-ranging, and at times seemingly self-contradictory, statutory duties imposed by s.3 (1) of the 1965 Act. Though the terms of the 1965 Act oblige the commissioners to act 'with a view [...] in particular [to] the codification' of Scots law, and the modernisation thereof, it is thought rather that the overarching prerogative of the SLC is to further the 'systematic development' of the law. Expressly, as a part of this, specifically 'the reduction of the number of separate enactments and generally the simplification' of the law is mandated by the terms of the governing legislation. Consequently, in recognition of the observation of Birks that there are in fact many 'different ways of reducing the incidence of confusion in the law',[32] and the passing of new legislation is in fact but one (blunt) instrument which may be employed for this task, it is thought that the connection between law reform and statutes is functionally overstated. The better tool for the task of bringing coherence to the law – in fact, what Birks considered to be 'the best' – starts by 'tak[ing] a lesson from the natural scientists and [...] pay[ing] attention, as they do, to taxonomy'.[33] The law should not be 'throw[n] together in any order that [comes] to hand',[34] nor should it be fractured into disparate, piecemeal rules stemming from several enactments passed by Parliaments across a plethora of years. Rather, law ought to be organised according to 'a system which rationally relate[s] together all of the parts of the law, much as a grammar relates together the diverse elements of a language'.[35] Codification is not required to realise this goal and piecemeal codification is in fact antipathical to it.

Ultimately, then, this chapter proceeds – as does this book as a whole – from the premiss that legislation is not an unalloyed good and, indeed, that statutory intervention which displaces 'fixed and known Custome'[36] may be actively harmful to the desiderata of 'furthering the systematic development' of the law. To wit, it is proposed that the SLC – drawing on the expertise of its commissioners, the support of its research assistants and the benefits of its 'time-rich', open-ended, multipurpose constitution – is extremely well placed to contribute towards the production of a systemic understanding of Scots law resting – as the tradition historically has – on 'overview literature' rather than inflexible top-down legislation.[37] This, it is thought, would have many advantages. To adapt the words of Birks, a 'systematic' which remains 'constantly open to discussion and review' provides 'stability and a foundation for analysis and reflection without inhibiting improvement' as would a 'rigidified' code which would invariably 'impede subsequent criticism and innovation'.[38] Scots law, at one time, 'might [...] have congratulated itself on a notable, and notably valuable, asset', but even 30 years ago this asset was in the process of being 'frittered away'.[39] Nonetheless, though it would necessitate a marked culture change, and a reconsideration of the overarching duties of the commissioners in their quest to effect law reform, presently those commissioners are in fact uniquely placed to strengthen 'the advantage which the long overview tradition conferred on Scots law'.[40] Working in tandem with law teachers, and drawing on the lessons imparted by institutional writers such as Stair, Bell and others, it is believed that the SLC might allow Scots law to achieve a 'higher rationality' and that effective reform may be realised without either a proliferation of piecemeal legislation or, for that matter, wholesale codification of the legal framework.

Watson's 'General Thesis' and Its Consequences

Watson was of the view that his 'general thesis' – that rulers are not typically interested in the content of the laws by which their subjects are governed – could be substantiated with reference to 'facts that [...] no serious legal scholar would consider denying, but which are not usually considered together'.[41] These facts are that in the formative period of Roman law ('the most innovative [and influential] [system of jurisprudence] the world has ever known'),[42] developments in law and legal change were spearheaded, led and brought to pass by the jurists; private individuals with no (necessary or formal) ties to government or the state.[43] When Roman law was received in Western Europe, from the outset of the system's 'second life', the reception was headed, again, by private individuals with no (necessary or formal) ties to any state or government;[44] in a word, jurists (albeit in possession of an altogether distinct methodology from that of their Roman forebears),[45] this time in the guise of professors at the emergent universities.[46] Jurists of this sort contributed considerably to the development of the (distinctly non-Roman) feudal law as well as that of the received *ius Civile* and municipal law (to say nothing of the 'law of nature and nations', the *ius naturae et gentium*),[47] long after the societal and military feudal system itself had functionally ceased to retain practical relevance.[48]

The crucial factor which allowed these private individuals to shape the law through their learned writings was the relative paucity of legislation on private law during the relevant, formative periods. This general absence is not, as Watson notes, due to any lack of practical power or authority to legislate (indeed it is misleading to confuse the ability to enforce legislation with the ability to pass it),[49] since 'the same times and places saw much legislation on other matters'.[50] The real reason for the absence of such legislation, it would seem, is the fact that 'European rulers have often been indifferent to communicating clearly the substance of law, even of criminal law, to their subjects' and even where rulers who are concerned with improving the 'accessibility' of the law emerge, the actual content of the promulgated rules tends to be of 'generally less concern'.[51] The Common law of England – 'haphazard, slow, unresponsive to social and political conditions, incomprehensible to non-lawyers and unsystematic'[52] as it is – could not have developed in the form that it did had the rulers of that Kingdom cared about the content of the 'royal law'.[53] That Scots law has historically been more systematic than the Anglo-American Common law (even if the charges of unresponsiveness and incomprehensibility may nonetheless be levied against Scots common law, along with the law of any other uncodified system)[54] is not attributable to the care and attention of any sovereign political decision-maker (indeed, Scots law

– being that Scotland lacked its own dedicated legislature circa. 1707–1999 – may be said to have been peculiarly neglected by 'the King in Parliament').[55] Rather, the Scottish 'commitment to [...] a more systematic approach'[56] is one which has its genesis in the fact that 'law' has been treated as a worthy subject of independent intellectual study in line with the Continental European, rather than parochial English, tradition,[57] thus allowing for the generation of learned works such as Stair's *Institutions* and Bell's *Commentaries* as well as – with the exception of a particularly arid period from the end of the First World War to the 1960s[58] – 'a large and growing body of excellent texts [...] a legal literature sufficient to service the legal system'.[59]

The SLC, with its conventional, practical and (ongoing) physical separation from government (both that of Whitehall or Holyrood; i.e., the political sovereign and/or the superior) is – though not completely independent of political oversight – probably about as 'independent as any government-funded public body can reasonably expect to be'.[60] Consequently, it and its commissioners can be identified as actors exhibiting similarities with the Roman jurists and Civilian professors of law in uncodified systems. They are concerned with rationalising the law and rendering it accessible, and, though not generally agnostic on policy (since such is practically impossible where legal change is concerned), they are involved with the technical detail of particular aspects of jurisprudence in an essentially 'apolitical' way. Nonetheless, unlike those other, principally private, independent individuals who have concerned themselves with the intellectual discipline of law,[61] the Scottish law commissioners find themselves in something of a double-bind due to the burdensome duties imposed on such office-holders by the constitutive statute – the Law Commissions Act 1965 – as well as a more direct relationship to government than jurists have typically had hitherto, at a time in which the Scottish government has displayed an enthusiasm for legislation (if not terribly much interest in the content thereof). The activities of the SLC having state sanction – even arm's length state sanction – also means that the commissioners can count on the possibility of legislation to bring about their desired reforms in a way that, traditionally, jurists who seek to rationalise law within the confines of already-existing *ius* cannot.[62] Against this background, it is unsurprising that 'over the years the inclusion of a [draft] bill [appending any given SLC report] gradually became the norm'.[63]

Yet legislation is but one way of 'reducing the incidence of confusion in the law' and it is not necessarily the best way.[64] Indeed, as has been said but must be stressed, a proliferation of piecemeal legislation can leave the law as (if not in fact more) uncertain and inaccessible as can a dearth of authoritative declarations from a sovereign or superior decision-maker.[65] Reducing confusion in the law, and rendering accessible the complex and arcane, is one of the principal duties of the law teacher, but more than that it is a prime prerogative of the law commissioner and, indeed, must be taken to be a key desiderata of any system of justice. As indicated in the introduction, Birks notes that a particularly useful way of reducing confusion in the law is through the systematisation of jurisprudence; this can only be done, though, by those willing to pay attention to taxonomy and the overarching structure of the legal framework. Here, Scots lawyers have an advantage over their Common law colleagues, since there has long been, in Scotland, a tradition of overview literature engaging with the whole of the law as an ordered and systemic subject of intellectual study. This overview literature – the so-called 'Institutional writings' – was written 'according to a system which rationally related together all the parts of the law, much as a grammar relates together the diverse elements of a language'.[66]

As was observed in the introduction to the present short book, the Westminster Parliament was originally reluctant to extend the remit of the Law Commissions Act 1965 to Scotland, due to the fact that the legal framework of this jurisdiction was already in large part rational and ordered (or at least capable of being treated as such), in the absence of legislation or express codification, because of this overview literature.[67] The reasons why the 1965 Act was nonetheless extended to this jurisdiction have been explored at length elsewhere[68] and there is little doubt that the creation of the SLC was something of an afterthought. Indeed, as Wilson-Stark has indicated, it is clear that certain contemporary Scots, such as the then Lord Advocate and Secretary of State for Scotland, were sceptical even of the vision for the Law Commission for England and Wales – albeit that they ultimately colluded to facilitate the creation of an independent SLC more 'out of a sense of institutional necessity, rather than a burning desire for Scots law reform'.[69] As Gretton observed, 'if there had been just one commission' – whether for England and Wales only, or a 'Great British' commission[70] – then presently the laws of Scotland and England would be 'much more assimilated than they in fact are'.[71] This assimilation almost certainly would have been along the lines of English, rather than Scots, law which would have been most regrettable from the standpoint of any proponent of legal rationality and order.

As it stands, the existence of separate commissions – and indeed, perhaps, the position of the infamously pro-Civilian and inimitably energetic T. B. Smith as one of Scotland's first commissioners[72] – has done much to preserve Scotland's unique legal culture and developmental history. Indeed, it is perhaps notable that in the abortive project to codify the law of 'contract' for the whole of the United Kingdom, the draft material which had been produced to facilitate the introduction of such a code had 'moved [...] substantially in the direction of Scots law, as by proposing abolition of the doctrine of consideration and recognition of the rights of third parties', among other things, by the time that it was abandoned.[73] Commenting on his role *vis* this project, Smith – as a then serving commissioner – was prevented by protocol 'from twitching aside the veil of confidentiality and revealing Truth starkly naked',[74] but broadly endorsed the understanding of the difficulties encountered in the course of the project as articulated by his English commission counterpart Laurence Gower: 'The difficulties [in the codification project did not arise] because the English and the Scots disagree[d] on results, but because we speak different legal languages and arrive at the results by a different process of reasoning. And to those trained in the more philosophical "Civilian" school the process of reasoning is more sacred than it is to the Common lawyer.'[75]

A particular sticking point arose in respect of the enforceability of unilateral undertakings. *Per* Gower,

> 'both we and the Scots agreed that, in certain circumstances at any rate, a unilateral promise not supported by consideration should be enforceable [...]. I wanted to achieve this by defining a contract so that it would include such promises. But my opposite number on the Scottish Law Commission would have none of this. A *pollicitatio*, he said, was an enforceable voluntary obligation but it was not a contract and to pretend that it was would sap the very foundations of sound principle. To me that did not matter so long as we achieved the desired result; to him it was unthinkable.'[76]

In the words of MacQueen, Gower here manifestly demonstrated 'the characteristic willingness of English law to force distinct factual situations into categories which are then made unnecessarily wide and difficult to understand and apply'.[77] Smith, however, demonstrated the 'determined rationality' that one would expect of a Scots jurist; indeed, 'the [clear] separation of promise from contract had been a major [...] achievement of Smith's writing'[78] albeit that the distinction was, as indicated in the first chapter of this book, expressed quite plainly by Stair some three hundred years prior.

Nonetheless, though these 'differences in thought processes and vocabulary make unification [of the laws of Scotland with the rest of the United Kingdom] extraordinarily difficult',[79] there can be little doubt that there were by the 1960s (and that there remain in 2025) strong similarities in the philosophical idea of what 'law' is,[80] how it is made and how it subsists – including a ranking of a hierarchy of positive sources of law[81] – even if Scotland and England continued to differ in matters of doctrinal detail (and even if philosophical thought traditionally diverged).[82] As McCall Smith, writing in 1976, observed 'at the moment Scots law is very much more of a Common law system than it is a Civilian, and the impact of substantive English law and the reception by the Court of Session of the doctrine of precedent would indicate a more appropriate positioning within the Anglo-American tradition'.[83] The solution, in his view (considering the 'unsatisfactory aspects of having to refer to writers who precede even 19th-century legal science [to determine and identify the underlying principles of Scots law] [...] self-evident'),[84] was codification – a view which accords with Lord Scarman's declared 'commit[ment] to the codification of English law as a principal instrument of law reform'[85] and is consistent with the SLC's initial commitment to the codification of Scots.[86]

The above is not merely consistent with the idea of a 'reception' of English legal doctrine, law and thought into Scots,[87] but also correlates with 'the hypothesis of a specific revolution between the Eighteenth and Twentieth centuries that affected the whole world' put forth by Dupret and Parolin in a recent study.[88] This intellectual revolution was, in their words, 'characteristic of a Great Divide [...] between an Ancient and a New legal Regime'.[89] The hypothesised division is one which straddled the traditional separation of Common and Civilian jurisprudence and was a decidedly pan-European phenomenon,[90] albeit one exported across the globe as a result of Western imperialism, as well as European nations' colonial connections to the rest of the planet.[91] The phenomenon – and resulting 'break point' – is termed the 'positivisation of the law' by Dupret and Parolin, 'referring to the gradual rise in importance of "legal positivism", so well described by English jurist John Austin, who tended to equate the "law properly so called" with the rules emanating from the sovereign command of the state'.[92]

The positivism of Austin and his successors (as well as Austin's forebear, Pufendorf)[93] 'though purporting to be an observation [...] is best viewed as a dogma, which derives basically from viewing all law in terms of a model of statute law'.[94] In refuting any essential connection between law and morality, contemporary legal positivism elevates law in the sense of *lex* (declaration) – more particularly, statute – to the supreme position of 'law properly so-called' and struggles to accommodate the idea of custom (and so, by extension, non-statutory 'common law' – which 'grows up', rather than being 'handed-down') to the status of law absent some sanction from a 'state official' seen to be exercising some particular role (such as that of 'judge'). The positivisation of law can, on one view, be viewed as a serious intellectual advancement, a 'great leap forward'. Indeed, 'the insistence that all law is legislated law makes possible the view that all law is changeable' and this was said by MacCormick to be 'an essential postulate for those who wish to reform the law'.[95] This – as is explored further below – is not entirely true in an unqualified sense (law can, it is submitted, be reformed without being remade or recast by or in statute), but it is certainly the case that the idea that the law is protean and alterable at the whim of the legislator is a necessary prerequisite of the codification of a system's jurisprudence and, if codification is regarded as a virtue, positivisation must be so also.[96]

Although the positivisation of law might be viewed as a desirable intellectual advance (and, indeed, this point of view might be said to be the prevalent orthodoxy of the twenty-first century), it is nonetheless postulated that while the idea of a protean and changeable – fundamentally positivised law – may allow for, if not lead to, the wholesale codification of a given system's jurisprudence, it is more likely that in the absence of a health body of juristic literature such will instead lead to an uncontrolled, and undesirable, proliferation of positive 'sources of law' – up to and including primary legislation – rather than the production of a rational and juristically satisfactory code. The position of Roman law following the eclipse of the classical jurists, but before the reforms spearheaded by Justinian, is telling in this regard. So-called 'Roman legal science' had conventional opinion holds, fallen into a sorry state by the time of the later period of the Dominate.[97] Private commentaries on the law at this time were 'to a great extent limited to elementary texts, including collections and summaries of classical texts'.[98] Yet the extent to which the shift – as it is undoubted that there was a shift – from classical to post-classical law was significant can be and has been questioned.[99] Indeed, the 'positivisation' of the 'authority' of a *numerus clausus* of classical jurists effected by Valentinian III's *Lex Citationum* of 426 CE 'is not very different from the system of binding precedent that is applied in Scottish and English courts' and though undoubtedly 'artificial, mechanical and not conducive to coherent legal development'[100] mirrors, albeit in a far more stark and naked manner, the positivisation of the Scottish institutional writers as a formal 'source of law'.[101] Hence, while it has been said that the post-classical, pre-Justinianic period was not 'an old age of mere decrepitude' and that 'its stagnation […] [has] been greatly exaggerated; it was still capable of carrying on important reforms which were genuine developments along the line of its own proper traditions',[102] there is a reason why the period of the classical jurists – attempting to discern 'what is right' through application of reason – is regarded as the 'high water mark' of Roman jurisprudence and the font of equity that came to inform the development of jurisprudence in the *ius commune*.[103]

By the time Justinian ascended the throne, however, 'the mere bulk of the statute law was a serious obstacle to its application in practice';[104] altering the law, and creating new laws, was seen to be in the gift of the sovereign, which unlike in the heyday of the classical jurists was keen to exercise its faculty of effecting legal change with scant regard for the coherence of 'the law' as a whole or (consistent with Watson's general thesis) the precise content of the individual *leges* passed in its name. Faced with the 'great chaotic masses' of unquestionably authoritative legislation and questionably authoritative declarations of 'that which is right',[105] wholesale codification – which may involve the simplistic and unsatisfactory 'transplanting' of unsuitable foreign law[106] as well as arbitrarily picking a solution proffered by one side or the other in a given disputed topic and elevating this to the status of *lex* – may come to be seen as preferable to the *status quo*. Such is evidenced, in the Roman context, by the efforts of Theodosius II who promulgated the *Codex Theodosianus* (incorporating the *Lex Citationum* of his Western contemporary, Valentinian III) to improve the 'accessibility' of the law, without taking terribly much care for reform of its content. Presently, in respect of Scots law, the impetus to legislate holistically, without too much care for the quality of the 'law' expressed in the code, has been expressed by MacQueen (a former Scottish law commissioner): 'A code – or quasi-codifying statutes in particular areas – would at least have the merit of stating authoritatively what the law is, for good or ill.'[107]

This view expressed by MacQueen here accords with the irritation expressed by Hogg, who has decried the amount of 'academic time [...] spent in forensic investigation of what the law is, and in writing articles which laboriously trace the correct path of legal development through Nineteenth Century and earlier case law'.[108] He has admitted to becoming 'increasingly frustrated over the course of [his] own career by the amount of time [he] ha[s] had to spend in writing articles in which [he] ha[s] tried to argue that particular rules ought to be the position in Scots law, or [...] that certain fundamental words used by our legal system to describe the nature of obligations should mean x or y'.[109] Resultantly, he has long 'gaze[d] enviously upon other country's Civil Codes in which these matters are set out in a few lines', which ensure that within such systems there are 'no hours of wasted time for academics [...] arguing repeatedly about what the position should be'.[110]

In this, the views of MacQueen, Hogg and perhaps Theodosius II may be said to align with the view of Lord Mansfield – a Scots-born, English-qualified judge and himself a close associate of Lord Kames[111] – that it is generally of 'more importance in most cases that the law should be certain than what the law is'.[112] Mansfield's account further accords with that of his friend, Lord Kames, who observed that 'general rules, it is true, must often produce decrees that are materially unjust; for no rule can be equally just in its application to a whole class of cases [...] but this inconvenience must be tolerated, to avoid a greater, that of making judges arbitrary'.[113] The appeal of this view is manifest and has been taken up and defended by judicial figures even in systems heavily influenced by the rationalising tendencies of the

Civil law tradition[114] – albeit one operating during the 'dark days' of South African apartheid.[115] The extremes to which this overtly positivistic approach to law may be stretched are, it is thought, such that the desirability of certain rigid 'bad' law must necessarily be rejected. That is not, in and of itself, an argument for maintaining uncertainty in the law; it merely feeds into the broader argument that it is in the interests of justice, in its broad sense, that the 'right' answer to legal problems be deduced from ordered principle rather than through inflexible doctrinal rulings or declarations. Indeed, as Watson observed, 'the ability and readiness of society to tolerate inappropriate private law is truly remarkable [...]. Lawyers in fact have exaggerated the role of private law rules in promoting the well-being and happiness of society; society's essential stake in these rules is the avoidance or settlement of conflict, and for that their quality is of secondary importance'.[116]

While, then, MacQueen suggests that if piecemeal legislative reform 'turn[s] out to be ill, it could then be reformed with better understanding of what the problems for solution are',[117] and the existence of Scotland's own devolved legislature in theory if not in practice allows such rectification to be effected speedily,[118] one must bear in mind Watson's warning and recognise that practically the wheels of law reform move very slowly indeed. While the position adopted by Hogg and MacQueen may serve as an *apologia* for continental European-style codification in Scotland, it would be a crass understatement to say that the prospects of such holistic codification in such a jurisdiction are functionally impossible. As the erstwhile Chair of the Scottish Law Commission – Lord Hunter – observed in 1988, 'codification in anything like the Continental sense must be a pipedream so long as the methods of drafting and processing legislation in the Westminster [and, indeed – post-devolution – Holyrood] Parliament[s] take their present form and so long as the methods of interpretation of statutes by courts in this country remain [...] unchanged'.[119]

In the absence of overarching Continental-style codification, therefore, meaningful legislative law reform must necessarily lead to either the retrograde fragmentation of principled categories of jurisprudence (such as the law of property and obligations) into discrete free-standing topics or a proliferation, rather than a reduction, of the number of specific enactments. This, essentially, places the Law Commissioners in a double-bind as they are obliged to simultaneously codify and simplify, but any proliferation of enactments must necessarily compound complexity rather than facilitating ease of understanding and accessibility. Caught, as they are, in this double-bind, it may be suggested that legislative inaction rather than action is to be preferred; any given area of law may well need reform, but more satisfactory reform might be brought about by leaving jurisprudential reform to the courts and jurists (and – a point which will be returned to – the SLC itself is comprised of 'jurists') – at least for a time – before declaring an unequivocal (and perhaps faulty) rule via statute.

Hogg himself recognises this. Although he himself stands as something of an advocate for wholesale codification, he nonetheless acknowledged that 'if one decides on a solution to a problem for the purposes of codifying it, one better get the solution right'.[120] MacQueen, for his part, acknowledges the desirability of getting 'the law' right, but his optimism that problems created by legislation may simply be solved by legislation overlooks the possibility that more basic, structural problems caused by legislation might not be solvable through the introduction of further statute. A vase, once smashed, can be put back together but will henceforth – even if only subtly – bear the marks of its destruction. To put matters less poetically and more practically, we should consider two observations – one made by Watson, the other by Stair. The first is that legislation 'can break entirely with the existing tradition and even, in theory, with any legal tradition [and] remake the whole of a legal system'.[121] The second is Stair's observation that 'in Statutory Written Law, the Vestige of all the alterations remain';[122] once a *lex* declares that the pre-existing common law is abolished, it is consequently difficult to see how – in this overtly positivistic age – the learning that led to the development of that common law could be revived. Consequently, while centuries or millennia of legal learning can cease to have relevance at the stroke of a pen, once this path is settled on it cannot really be undone with the same amount of ease. Hence, though statutory reforms such as those effected by the Contract (Rights of Third Parties) (Scotland) Act 2017, or that which would be brought to bear by the Contract (Formation) Scotland Bill, can radically change the law overnight, the ill-effects produced by such statutes could not be undone at the stroke of a pen even if the legislator were minded to revisit an issue of 'technical law reform' having recently posited a statute on that given topic.

While, then, the view that problems arising from the *status quo* of legal uncertainty and disorder may be solved through legislative intervention, even what appears to be relatively minor statutory intervention,[123] is attractive because it has the benefit of 'declaring the law' plainly and making it known, according nicely with the positivistic orthodoxy of the present age, legislative intervention is no panacea to the problems of unsatisfactory law. Indeed, the proliferation of piecemeal statutes, and the view that only declarations emanating from sovereign or superior 'lawgiver' deserve the appellation of 'law properly so-called' is not merely unconducive to the development of rational legal order, it is actively detrimental to it. The application of juristic reason to concrete fact-patterns – which is a pursuit that only those learned in the heuristics of law can engage in effectively[124] – combined with the application of the faculty of pattern-recognition to allow for the articulation of a clear and rational taxonomy, is (perhaps unsurprisingly) more conducive to the production of quality law than is the uncontrolled proliferation of discrete and fragmented *leges* (whether in the form of legislation, judicial precedent or any other such source) or the promulgation of a code which prizes harsh certainty over juristic quality.

The SLC is, it might be thought, almost uniquely placed to contribute to the revitalisation of the kind of 'overview literature' which is needed to anchor juristic reasoning in particular cases to a wider, rational system of law (in the sense of *ius*). From the outset of the creation of the twin commissions, however, there has existed the idea that the SLC stands as but an advisor to the sovereign or superior, within whose province the true faculty of law reform falls.[125] Lord Scarman, for instance, considered that 'the Commission [stands] committed to the codification of English law as a principal instrument of law reform'[126] and what is said here of English law is true, *mutatis mutandis*, for Scots law via the SLC. Yet while one might say that the primary function of the SLC is to 'assist the Government or Parliament [whether at the Scottish or UK level], first in the planning of law reform',[127] the second core objective of the SLC – 'the formulation of proposals for the systematic development and reform of the law'[128] – may be realised by legislation, but crucially *need* not be. If one considers, for instance, the SLC project on contractual third-party rights, which resulted in the creation of the 2017 Act, MacQueen (the lead commissioner for this project) himself recognised that the topic was 'an area of essentially judge-made law, the problems with which could conceivably be sorted out by the courts themselves'.[129] For the courts to achieve this, however, 'the right case would have to emerge and its potential significance be recognised by advisers, pleaders and judges, while the parties would also have to be ready, financially and in other aspects, to take it all the way to the Supreme Court to have a previous decision of the House of Lords over-turned'.[130] One can only agree with MacQueen's assessment that 'the chances of all these things occurring simultaneously in a small legal system are, however, remote indeed'.[131]

Rather than seeking to resolve the matter by legislative fiat, however, it is here submitted that the nature of the SLC – as a law reform body staffed by eminently qualified jurists, headed up by a senior judge of the Inner House of the Court of Session,[132] and generally respected by the legal profession and judiciary – is manifestly capable of effecting significant, rational, law reform and legal change through means other than simply persuading the legislature to Act. Indeed, that they have been able to do so is evidenced by, for example, the judgement of the Court of Session in *Glasgow City Council v. The Board of Managers of Springboig St John's School*,[133] in which – drawing on the Scottish Law Commission's 2006 discussion paper on the *Nature and the Constitution of Trusts*[134] – it was found that the dual patrimony theory of the Scottish trust 'explain[s] the protection of trust property held by a trustee against claims by the trustee's personal creditors'.[135] This indicates that – as a source of legal writing – the discussion papers, reports, memoranda and other outputs of the SLC have, in and of themselves, the potential to influence the development of the law, even in the absence of enabling legislation. Indeed, in the case of the report on trusts, it may in fact be that the legislation passed, as a result of the recommendations of the literature concerning that project, actively undermines the rationality of the law, in that area, as articulated in the juristic material.[136] Ultimately, then, it is here submitted that although the impetus for the SLC to agitate for legislative law reform is understandable, for cultural and pragmatic reasons alike, there are manifestly other – indeed, it is here submitted better – avenues for the commission to effect rational, intellectually satisfactory, law reform, avenues which, in fact, the SLC already pursue. While it is the case that something of a culture change – away from the overtly positivistic conception of law which abides in Scotland, as in England and elsewhere in the Western world today – would be necessary to realise the full potential of SLC reforms which do not result in or urge the passing of legislation, as the next section of this chapter indicates, the requisite culture change would not need to be as dramatic as it might ostensibly appear at first sight. It involves, simply, a re-analysis – perhaps one might say a re-discovery – of the meaning of 'legal authority' within the context of the Scottish legal tradition.

Law Reform, Legal Authority and Legal Rationality

The terms of the Law Commissions Act 1965 'are [...] breathtakingly wide',[137] placing all of the law of Scotland within the purview of the SLC.[138] As the first head of the Commission for England and Wales noted, 'this comprehensive approach is important; the Act gives the Law Commission wider terms of reference than any previous law reform agency has ever had and it enables it to consider proposals against the background of the law as a whole. A patchwork quilt of improvements unrelated to the whole pattern of the law is apt to create as many problems as it solves; each reform must be fitted into a coherent structure and this can only be achieved if the law reform agency has a general planning responsibility for the entire law.'[139] Seemingly from the outset of the establishment of the twin commissions, then, it seems that the wisdom of paying attention to taxonomy – something which has not, historically, been recognised by Common lawyers[140] – was appreciated as was, indeed, the utility of developing 'communications between the courts, the legislature and the public' insofar as even 'technical' law reform is concerned.[141]

The observations of Lord Scarman pertaining to the importance of legal rationality would likely be approved of by those 'learnedest lawyers', spoken of by Stair,[142] who have long counselled the cause of treating law as a rational discipline at once worthy of intellectual study as a subject in its own right and capable of logical, coherent expression.[143] The law, properly so called, ought to be discoverable, discernible and explicable through the application of human reason and thought;[144] the possibility of such, it may be submitted, marks the inescapable distinction between a system which operates under the rule of law as opposed to one which functions according to rule by law.[145] Nonetheless, the view that law ought to be rational, and capable of deduction, rather than merely being a *corpus* comprised of an emergent body of norms or rules handed down from on high is now decidedly unfashionable. With that said, it seems that it was ever thus: In the seventeenth century, on venturing to ask 'whether Law may, or should be handled as a rational discipline, having principles from whence its Conclusions may be deduced', Stair immediately conceded that most lawyers are and ever have been 'for the negative part'.[146] Their reasons for this view are multitudinous and to an extent understandable; as articulated by Stair, most esteem 'law, especially the positive and proper Laws of any Nation, incapable of such a[ny rational] deduction, as being dependent upon the will and pleasure of Law-givers, and introduced for Utilities sake, and so frequently alterable, that they cannot be drawn from prior common Principles, and keep the artificial method of rational Disciplines; and therefore they rest satisfied with any order'.[147]

Yet though most lawyers (and so, it must be inferred, the overwhelming preponderance of laypersons) may be of the view that 'law' is ultimately irrational, reducible to political expediency and best expressed in the form of clear – if piecemeal – rules handed down from a sovereign decision-maker, it is a common refrain that 'the learnedest Lawers [...] have thought it both feasible and fit, that the Law should be formed as a Rational Discipline, and have much regrated that it hath not been effectuated'.[148] Indeed, within Justinian's Digest, the essential connection between 'law' and 'rules' – central to much modern legal philosophy, particularly that flowing from the positivist school of Austin,[149] Kelsen,[150] Hart[151] and their successors[152] – is not merely doubted, but actively disavowed: 'A rule is that which briefly explains the details of a thing. The law may not be arrogated from a rule, but a rule must be made from the law as it is. For a rule, consequently, gives a brief narration of the thing and, so Sabinus says, it is like an outline of the case, which as soon as it is corrupted in any way, is deprived of service.'[153] In effect, then, rather than 'law' standing as a collation or aggregate of disparate 'rules', for the Romans (and by extension their immediate juristic successors at least) 'rules' were in fact pedagogical tools employed to pithily express a recognised principle arising out of the 'law' – that 'law' itself recognised as the art of arriving at the 'right' – as in 'correct'[154] – decision in any given practical dispute[155] (the correct decision in any case being, essentially, that which 'gives to each his due').[156]

The view expressed by Paulus, as adopted by Justinian – perhaps ironically, given the historical propensity of certain English lawyers to boast that the jurisprudence of the Common law developed in 'splendid isolation' from the Continental European *ius commune* (including Scotland)[157] – corresponds with the reality of the law that emerged out of the early English royal courts.[158] That is to say, for much of English legal history, essentially prior to the emergence of a rigid doctrine of *stare decisis*,[159] judges were not and indeed could not be conceptualised as 'legislators' or 'quasi-legislators' (as they were for Austin[160] and tacitly are for his juristic successors also).[161] In the early English law, as indeed in early Scots law, the prevalent view was that law – other than that authoritatively handed down by the sovereign in the fashion of some *lex*[162] (and *leges* of this kind, in Scotland at least, are liable to fall into desuetude)[163] – was discovered rather than made anew by officials. Hence, Stein describes the situation thus: 'When a case arises for which no valid law can be adduced, then the lawful men or doomsmen [would] make [a] new law in the belief that what they are making is good old law, not indeed expressly handed-down, but tacitly existent. They do not, therefore, create the law, they discover it.'[164]

In any system which conceives of 'law' in this way – and history teaches us that this is not the only valid perspective on the nature of law, just as the popular positivism of our present age is not the only possible perspective[165] – 'what is right' may be either declared or undeclared. It is taken, as a matter of 'institutional fact',[166] that what 'is correct' in any particular case is, and always has been, known by all (even if, as a matter of brute fact outwith the artifice of legal reality, the authoritative declaration of 'what is right' by a decision-maker – such as a judge – comes as a surprise to all and sundry, as well as to the particular party who lost their case).[167] Naturally, given that 'law, whether it is regarded as already existing and simply to be discovered, or made by preceding conscious human determination, or to be made during the instant case, has to achieve some express linguistic formulation',[168] and any such linguistic formulation can broadly be understood as a declaration (and so *lex* rather than *ius*) the question of the 'authority' (or lack thereof) of that particular formulation is begged. Watson suggests that a formulation 'is authoritative when it is treated by the courts as resting on a basis which the courts habitually regard as determinative for their decisions', noting that 'such bases differ from time to time and from place to place'.[169]

Given the supremacy of the caste of judges in the Common law tradition,[170] in contradistinction to the position in the *ius commune* (and Scotland – though as a 'mixed' jurisdiction it is something of a special case)[171] wherein the word of what can broadly be construed as 'academic lawyers' as 'authoritative' has consistently been recognised,[172] the emergence of a school of thought which sees judges conceptualised as legislators (or at least quasi-legislators) is understandable. Members of this class do not merely opine: they declare, authoritatively (and in actual cases, with immediate real-world consequences),[173] what is right and their declarations are treated in turn, by subsequent judges, who themselves put forth authoritative declarations, as authoritative (if not conclusive) statements of 'what is right'.[174] Within the Common law tradition (particularly given the centrality of the King, as sovereign figure, within that tradition),[175] consequently, *leges* are declared by the sovereign but also in this system *ius* is not available to be discerned by anyone with the inclination (as well as time and funds) to do so, through reference to objective reason or deduction as a rational discipline, but rather by a closed and cloistered caste who exercise their role at the behest of the Crown.[176] The declarations of 'that which is right' posited by judges, forming as they do the basis of subsequent judicial decisions, can readily be conceptualised as akin to *leges*; *per* Stein 'once a *lex* had been enacted, it recorded the law authoritatively and was intended to be as permanent as the *ius* which it stated'.[177] On the emergence or reception of a rigid doctrine of *stare decisis*, the superior courts, empowered as they are to bind lower courts in a fashion akin to legislation, do indeed appear to stand as quasi-legislators.[178]

Hence, on this conceptualisation, 'the legislature's is a supreme, the judges' a subordinate or derivative, power; in so far as custom and precedent function as sources of law, they do so by virtue of a tacit command of the legislature'.[179] It remains the case, however, that (as Simpson emphasises) 'creating a precedent is not the same thing as laying down the law'.[180] Rather than legislating, judges provide reasons for interpreting the law in a certain way, and in turn – by virtue of their office and recognised expertise – subsequent judges pay due accord to these previous interpretations of certain points. As Smith put it, 'The higher the degree of generality [...] the greater the role of the judicial interpreter. However, "the law" rather than judicial interpretation must in the end prevail.'[181] These corresponding views of two great jurists correspond with the concept of law as Stair would have understood it; *per* MacCormick, 'for Stair, doing justice according to law means simply adjudicating in accordance with principles of right reason, especially as evidenced by the long custom of the realm'.[182] 'Justice' may be taken to be done in the courts, for it is the function of courts to determine 'that which is right' in any given case – but the decision of a given court is not axiomatically 'right' and though undoubtedly a court decision may be taken to be an 'authoritative' indication of what is right in like cases, a past court decision cannot be treated as generating a 'conclusive' indication of what is right in such cases.[183]

In indicating 'that which is right' in a given case, courts generate reasons – indeed, authoritative reasons – for inferring that their indication of 'that which is right' should be followed in like cases; not merely because like cases should be treated alike, but because all cases should be decided in accordance with law – in accordance with 'that which is right'. As Michelon points out, however, 'having an authoritative reason does not mean that you need to abide by that reason, as other facts might be pulling in the opposite direction'.[184] The issue of when given judicial decisions are to be understood 'binding' can be taken to be largely resolved within Scotland, but though the jurisdiction now has a recognised hierarchy of 'sources of law', it may yet be that 'there is nothing to compel [at least the senior] Scottish judges to accept any rule which offends their sense of justice, or which would subject them to servile compliance with recognised errors in policy or interpretation propounded by those who may now – too late – repent of them in the light of fuller understanding'.[185] Not only may Scottish judges act contrary to the reasons expressed by their fellow judges in interpreting 'that which is right' in a given case,[186] but by virtue of the equitable jurisdiction of the supreme Scottish courts,[187] the disapplication of statutes of the (supposedly otherwise 'sovereign')[188] Westminster Parliament may in certain circumstances be ordered.[189] Consequently, in the particular context of Scotland, judicial precedent may be thought of as a highly unsatisfactory source of the generation of *indicia* of how 'the law' is to be understood. The below passage, in the words of Watson, speaking of seventeenth- and eighteenth-century Scots law, though heavily truncated, thus merits serious consideration:

> Precedent was unsatisfactory as a major source of law. For the circumstances of the time it was unsatisfactory in that Scotland had a very small population and not enough cases to enable a clear picture of the law to emerge through precedent [...] [and it] was unsatisfactory in the way that it was handled for a variety of reasons. First, when judicial decisions were binding was not settled [...] secondly, the reports of cases are frequently overbrief and inadequate. The legal rule may not emerge from the report [...] The need for a further source of Scots law, which would fill gaps in the law and which would provide answers that could be argued to have some authority, is shown by the fact that from the date of publication Stair's *Institutions* themselves were cited in court, even though the concept of 'institutional writers' is much later.[190]

Though perhaps few would complain that modern case reports are 'overbrief', the charge of 'inadequacy' holds true in respect of (at least) some very notable cases of the twentieth and twenty-first centuries[191] and Scotland continues to maintain a small, relatively non-litigious populace. There is thus manifestly in our present day an imperious need for a source, other than precedent, which can generate authoritative *indicia* of how the law is to be interpreted, understood and applied and Parliament (whether in Holyrood or Westminster), as a legislative body, is for a host of reasons essentially unsuited to this task.[192] The 'third branch of the profession'[193] – the legal academy – might, as the institutional writers once did, fill this gap; indeed, the utility of the Scottish Universities Law Institute (SULI) and the publications arising from that series alone can hardly be overstated. They have been, and are, routinely cited in court[194] – however, it is notable that in some significant cases in which one would expect to see reference made to (at least) the leading SULI text, the courts have preferred the application of (even controverted and ostensibly unsatisfactory, on its own terms) English precedent.[195] Consequently – particularly in view of the rule of the Court of Session limiting the number of authorities which can be cited without special dispensation, but also due to the countervailing pressures of the positivisation of the concept of law – academics, unaided, are perhaps not best placed to stand (as they traditionally did in uncodified Civilian history) as the 'heroes' of modern Scots law (though they undoubtedly have a role to play, particularly as teachers).

The SLC, however, has a pool of technical expertise, is held in high esteem and enjoys a close connection to, but ultimate operational independence from, the 'sovereign or superior' legislator, which makes this body almost uniquely placed to 'fill gaps in the law and [...] provide answers that could be argued to have some authority'. In other words, then, the SLC is extremely well placed to inform and effect reform of the law without merely acting as a 'law reform activist body' akin to a privileged political pressure group, seeking to persuade an otherwise disinterested legislator to pass novel statutes dealing with this matter or that. While the first members of the twin law commissions manifestly recognised, as Lord Scarman did, that holistic consideration of 'the law' as a whole was imperative for the commissioners to adequately discharge their duties, as Gretton notes, since the halcyon days of the 1960s and 1970s 'patchwork reform has replaced the ideal of comprehensive redevelopment'.[196] To say that this is regrettable would be to mislead by understatement. A proliferation of statutes, as has been stressed, leads to legal uncertainty, which in turn may or may not lead to litigation, but in any case, where not plugged into the wider structure of the legal system, must necessarily lead to fragmentation and disorder. If the SLC is not *merely* concerned with 'codification' without due regard to the content of the given code (and it manifestly ought not to be, given the other duties of the commissioners), then the SLC, as a whole, must reckon with the fact that haphazard quasi-codification will invariably make the job of eventual holistic codification even more challenging than it presently is. By contrast, were the SLC to abstain from advocacy of arbitrary legislation to tackle bespoke topics, and instead set out its own authoritative (but ultimately inconclusive) statements of principle, bearing in mind the technicalities of any given area and their links to the wider legal framework, then over time the job of decidedly codifying the law – in a manner which, to paraphrase Hogg, 'gets the law right'[197] will be far easier.

Accordingly, although it has in recent decades preferred to simply advocate for piecemeal legislation to resolve discrete perceived problems in those areas which it is considered, the SLC can – and indeed, given the fact that it retains a duty to keep under review the whole of the law of Scotland, despite now being limited in its ability to influence and report to Westminster, arguably should – fulfil a role rather akin to that of the Scottish 'institutional writers' and conceivably be treated as such by the Scottish courts. *Per* Paisley, we in Scotland 'benefit greatly [...] from a system in which we have writers who write in a principled way and try and write about things which are not likely ever to come before the courts because they are, as it were, "under the bonnet", but with a view to assisting the development of the law institutional writers have set out these themes'.[198] The analogy of 'under the bonnet' law reform is in fact used by Gretton specifically (along with other colourful metaphors) in describing the work of the SLC;[199] the key point, however, is this. Certain solutions to legal problems, which have in the words of Lord Gill 'the hallmarks of good law',[200] also in his words 'produce more articles than cases'.[201] This, however, 'can be regarded as a feature of Scots law, not a bug'.[202] 'Scottish jurisprudence is not beholden to precedent for the development of her legal doctrine',[203] as the example of the positivised authority of the institutional writers shows.

Rather than viewing all law as the arbitrary plaything of parliaments and politicians, divined in part by a priestly caste known as the 'judges', it seems appropriate (particularly having regard to the etymology of *jus* and – by extension – 'justice') to regard 'law' as 'that which is right' in any given case, whatever a given temporal 'sovereign' or 'superior' may otherwise wish to claim. The SLC, with its considerable advantages and the authority of its learned expertise at its back, is not bound by the limitations of a court and need not consign itself to opining on real and live cases, nor to seeking to persuade a legislative body to solve perceived problems via statute. It is, instead, well placed to (and indeed bound to) 'keep under review all the law' of Scotland 'with a view to its systematic development and reform', in particular 'the elimination of anomalies [...] and generally the simplification and modernisation of the law'.[204] These objectives can be met without Parliamentary intervention; the literature produced by the SLC has, in its own right, the potential to be 'persuasive' in court and so shape the outcome of future court disputes.

Being written down and publicly available, such material may also allow those who are subject to law to obtain a rounded understanding of how the law is likely to develop in a particular area and how that particular area fits within the wider scheme of the legal framework itself. To achieve this, little more needs to be done than already occurs at present; rather than satisfying themselves with asking questions (as the SLC did in its 1993 report on 'contract formation'), the commissioners need only venture to attempt to answer them (as the present author did in the previous chapter). Were they to do so – though the law would not be rendered as 'certain' as it would be if a legislative *lex* were to be passed – then they would be contributing to the provision of legal 'stability and a foundation for analysis and reflection without inhibiting improvement'.[205] Such would not merely be consistent with the overarching tradition of Scottish jurisprudence,[206] but – it is here submitted – such would be conducive to the development of good, technical law. This, it is concluded, ought to be the prime prerogative of the Scottish Law Commissioner, who can and should be assisted in their endeavour by other 'technical' experts such as legal academics, practitioners and judges – with the legislator being called in only as the option of last resort.

Conclusion

The SLC – though perhaps resourced less well than certain commissioners and commentators would like – is much better placed than a single, relatively junior, academic to (1) identify areas of law which would benefit from reform; (2) discern principles of Scottish jurisprudence relevant to that area, bearing in mind the holistic context of the legal system itself; (3) contribute to the development of holistic 'overview literature' which pays attention to the 'whole of Scots law' and (4) influence the development of Scots law by providing authoritative reasons for judicial actors to accept those principles, as elucidated, as an accurate representation of the law. While the SLC has proven more than able to achieve (1) and (2), its perceived impetus of 'codification' and 'modernisation' has stymied its ability to realise (3) and (4). For over the past two decades, the SLC has proven more keen to facilitate the proliferation of piecemeal statutes designed to tackle particular perceived problems, rather than to consider the importance of the holistic reform and evolution of Scots law. Nonetheless, provided that the commissioners deign to answer, rather than merely ask, important technical questions (such as those concerning the prospective consequences of the 'postal acceptance rule'), the possibility that an ordered, structured and rational jurisprudence may be realised remains live.

The possibility is live because – notwithstanding the positivistic orthodoxy of modern, globalised society – the notion of 'legal authority' does not stem from legislative, or quasi-legislative, power and the concept of 'law' itself cannot be reduced to a mass of overlapping or interconnected 'rules'. Rather, 'law' – being intimately connected with the notion of 'justice'[207] – is today, as it ever has been, concerned principally with doing what is 'right' in any instance of dispute. An enquiry into what 'rules' should be taken to govern a particular dispute may shed light on what the 'right' solution is, but 'the law may not be arrogated from a rule, but a rule must be made from the law as it is. For a rule [...] as soon as it is corrupted in any way, is deprived of service'.[208] At best, a given 'rule', whatever its provenance, gives a 'reason' and *per* Michelon 'a reason is simply a fact that counts in favour of doing or believing something'. Such reasons will generally be imbued with what he termed 'theoretical authority',[209] though a statute, in the modern age and even in Scotland, will in almost all cases possess something more akin to the 'conclusive authority' (whereby the 'fact that counts in favour of doing or believing something [...] is simply the say-so of the authority')[210] of the kind envisaged by Simpson.[211]

Determining 'that which is right' by basic appeal to authority – as legislation (particularly on a positivist conception) essentially and invariably does – is not merely a recipe for 'bad law' but is a recipe for tyranny. The idea that the actual content of declared law is immaterial, but that its 'certainty' and provenance as the will of the sovereign is the salient factor in commanding respect for it seems to bear the hallmarks of rule by arbitrary fiat rather than the 'rule of law'. This is not something which should be tolerated by any who believe that law is and ought to be more than the mere exercise of political power. The alternative is to base law – and the impetus to follow law – on the exercise of right reason seeking to discern logical rationales for reaching judicial decisions (in the case of the courts) and believing that this-or-that is the law (in the case of, essentially, everyone else in society). The SLC, combining (unlike traditional academia) evident positive authority (due to its status as a body established by statute and the fact that its chair invariably sits as a judicial figure in the Supreme Courts of Scotland) with functional independence from government and the evident experience and technical expertise of its commissioners are well (if not uniquely)[212] placed 'to generate non-exclusionary practical reasons' for action or belief. That is to say, by virtue of its own reports, discussion papers and literature, the SLC presently has the opportunity to shape the law in a rational way, in rather the fashion envisaged (and complimented) by Birks in his exegesis of the exceptional virtues of the uncodified Scots legal system.[213]

None of this is to say that there is no place for legislation, or legislative reform, or for the SLC to advocate the introduction of such where it is deemed to be warranted. If one considers, for instance, the unsatisfactory state of the law broadly pertaining to 'moveable transactions' for much of Scottish history, the case for the introduction of the Moveable Transactions (Scotland) Act 2023, and its introduction of the registers of assignations and statutory pledges (*inter alia*), almost makes itself.[214] Where problems do not need a statutory solution, however – where, for instance, 'the problems [identified] […] could conceivably be sorted out by the courts themselves', the SLC should not jump to the conclusion that a statute is warranted. Rather, they could instead take the opportunity to suggest how the perceived issues might be resolved, so that if a court case which has the opportunity to do something so bold as 'overturn' a precedent of, say, the Appellate Committee of the House of Lords, or Inner House of the Court of Session, does arise, the court in question is furnished with a persuasive argument as to why this should or should not be done. In doing this, not only would the law – presently – develop in a rational fashion congruous with the history and tradition of Scots law, but the fact of doing so would mean that – should the decision to codify ever in fact be taken – the quality of the content of the final code can more readily be assured.

Notes

1 The SLC was formed in 1965 and the South African Law Reform Commission (SALRC) was established by the South African Law Reform Commission Act 1973. The Louisiana State Law Institute, though perhaps 'in many ways unlike the SLC', but nonetheless categorised by Gretton as akin to a Law Commission of sorts – dates to 1938. 1992 legislation to establish a law reform convention in Quebec – a famously bilingual mixed jurisdiction – was never brought into force. Canada has itself twice set up a federal law reform commission and twice abolished it. See Gretton, *Law Commissioning*, 121, 124, 128.

2 Gretton, *Law Commissioning*, 124.

3 Consider the question, ultimately answered in the positive, posed by David Hope, Lord Hope of Craighead, *Do We Still Need a Scottish Law Commission?* (2005) Edin. L. R. 10.

4 Gretton, *Law Commissioning*, 128.

5 I, like the current Chair of Comparative Law at the University of Oxford, am very much interested in the theoretical underpinnings of the law of trusts across jurisdictions. Nonetheless, like Professor Smith, I have little difficulty in admitting that many of the 'problems' that conceptual questions concerning trusts give rise to might be thought 'either unanswerable or uninteresting' by many lawyers, to say

nothing of the general public: See Lionel Smith, 'Stateless Trusts' in Lionel Smith (ed.), *The Worlds of the Trust* (Cambridge University Press, 2013), 96.

6 For the absurdity of speaking of 'lawyers' law', see ibid., 124.

7 It is inescapably true that just as 'politics has become more legalised' in Scotland since the establishment of the Devolved Scottish Parliament in 1999, so too is the case that the law in Scotland has become more politicised, and is interfered with by politicians and government figures, to a much greater degree, than was the case over the preceding three hundred years: James G. Kellas, 'Lawyers in Contemporary Scottish Politics: A New "Dundas Despotism"?' in Lindsay Farmer and Scott Veitch (eds), *The State of Scots Law* (Butterworth, 2001), 34. It is also a truism, as Lord Scarman observed, that 'reform of the law, even reform of so-called "lawyer's law", always involves a social judgement': Leslie Scarman, *The Law Commission* (1972) Anglo-American Law Review 31, 32.

8 The 'medium term' project examining the law of homicide, announced in the Tenth programme of law reform and continued into the Eleventh, is inescapable of interest to the public as well as being concerned with a matter of general public interest. Nonetheless, in this – as in respect of its other projects – the approach of the SLC to the subject matter is technical and juristic, rather than principally concerned with 'policy'.

9 Gretton, *Law Commissioning*, 127.

10 Watson, *Slave Law*, ch.1.

11 Ibid., at 1.

12 As Watson elsewhere observed, 'lack of interest in private law on the part of the legislature is harmful only to the extent that the other sources of law [do] not cover [other issues] adequately': Alan Watson, *Sources of Law, Legal Change and Ambiguity* (T&T Clark Ltd., 1985), 52.

13 The simplistic view that 'law' is that which is decreed by a sovereign decision-maker who will impose sanction for disobedience to his decreets may be immediately identified with the work of the English legal positivist John Austin, in his *Province of Jurisprudence Determined* (John Murray, 1832). *Per* Watson, it would be generally admitted that this is the 'seminal work [...] for British legal positivism', with H.L.A. Hart and his disciples and successors regarding Austin's work as the point of departure for their own theories of legal positivism: Watson, *Failures*, 108. Yet in the tradition which preceded the advent of modern legal positivism, and embedded firmly in the theories of, essentially, any and all natural lawyers who proceed from any theological basis (and this, invariably, includes Stair), is the centrality of 'the will or command' of a superior to any definition of law 'properly so-called'. Theological distinctions aside, however, for present purposes a central difference between the theories is that those adherents of Austinian and post-Austinian positivism (including Austin's juristic forebear Pufendorf) are principally concerned with law in the sense of *lex* (taken not merely – as Watson does in his commentary on positivism – as 'statute' but as an authoritative declaration which – by some measure of remove – has behind it the authority of the 'sovereign', or at least some 'superior' – so including judicial [but not arbitral] authority). By contrast, under the natural law theories, law need not merely be 'handed down' by a human superior, but may also 'grow up' through emergent custom. In theological natural law theories, such customs typically emerge and 'grow up' due to reason dictating that we follow the known laws of God pertaining to equity and right conduct. The construct of 'God' may, under

such theories, be replaced by other constructs such as, for example, 'human utility', 'the social contract' or Rousseau's concept of the 'general will'. Discussion of the cause of custom 'growing up' is beyond the scope of this short book: the point is that natural law theories (1) need not be theological and (2) more readily describe 'law' as it is in the world (accounting, as they do, for statute *and* custom) than do purely positivist theories. In this, the present author aligns with the view of Simpson, who identifies the tenets of positivism as closer in character to a dogma than a critical observation: A.W.B. Simpson, 'The Common Law and Legal Theory' in Simpson (ed.), *Oxford Essays in Jurisprudence: Second Series* (Clarendon Press, 1973), 80. Hence, there is much to commend the 'post-positivist' philosophy developed and articulated by D. Neil MacCormick in his *Law, State and Practical Reason* series (1999–2008); see generally Hector L. MacQueen, 'A Post-Positivist Outlook from the Thistle' in Neil Walker (ed.), *MacCormick's Scotland* (EUP, 2012), at 6: 'it is perhaps not too much of an exaggeration to say that by the end of his life Neil was seeking a rapprochement between positivism and natural law'. Such a rapprochement is, it is thought, more likely to shed light on the true nature of 'law properly so-called' than any one purist view.

14 Watson characterises the classical jurists as the 'heroes' of the Roman law proper, the continental professors as the 'heroes' of the (uncodified) Civilian tradition and the judges as the 'heroes' of the Common law. In like vein, law commissioners have the potential to effect rational legal change – so evolving to be 'heroes' of the given legal culture in which they are located: Watson, *Slave Law*, 3–4. It may be that codified jurisdictions (of whatever stripe) have no heroes, or perceive no need for them; Watson is silent on this point.

15 At least, according to the account given by Professor Reid – a former Scottish law commissioner – in the keynote delivered to the Young Property Lawyers Forum in 2019: Kenneth G.C. Reid, *Continuity and Change* (YPLF Lecture, University of Glasgow, 6 June 2019).

16 Ibid., 4. It must be borne in mind that within the English legal tradition, 'the elaboration of rules and principles governing the use of precedents and their status as authorities is relatively modern, and the idea that there could be binding precedents more recent still': Simpson, 'Legal Theory', 77.

17 Watson, *Slave Law*, 5.

18 In this regard, they are perhaps not dissimilar from the jurists of the later Roman Empire, 'work[ing] within a constitutional framework by which [legislation stands as] the most authoritative source of law': Tony Honoré, *Tribonian* (Bloomsbury, 1978), at xiv.

19 Ibid., 2.

20 Ibid.

21 Defamation and Malicious Publications (Scotland) Act 2021.

22 Moveable Transactions (Scotland) Act 2023.

23 Judicial Factors (Scotland) Act 2025.

24 Trusts and Succession (Scotland) Act 2024.

25 Consider, e.g., the criticisms of the reforms to Scots defamation law put forth in Stephen Bogle and Bobby Lindsay, *How Serious Is the Serious Harm Threshold?* (SSRN, Working draft - 22/3/24), at 8.

26 Gretton, *Law Commissioning*, 140.

27 *The Report on the Tenancy of Shops (Scotland) Act 1949* (2025) Scot. Law Co. 267.

28 The joint SLC–Law Commission reports on insurance contracts, automated vehicles and electoral law did not produce draft bills: in the case of the Electoral Law review (see 2020 Report 256: Electoral Law), though the Commissions themselves were willing to construct a draft (see para.1.7;1.21) and believed legislation to be warranted, 'the conception [...] of a single Act of the United Kingdom Parliament governing all elections within the scope of the project [...] bec[a]me outdated' during the lifespan of the project (para.1.22).

29 Gretton, *Law Commissioning*, 140.

30 See Wilson-Stark, *Origins*, 65.

31 Gretton, *Law Commissioning*, 127.

32 Birks, 'More Logic', 171.

33 Ibid.

34 Ibid., 171–172.

35 Ibid., 172.

36 To use the words of Stair, *Institutions*, I, 1, 15.

37 Birks, 'More Logic', 173.

38 Ibid.

39 Ibid.

40 Ibid., 174.

41 Watson, *Slave Law*, 1.

42 Ibid.

43 On the Roman jurists, see Gordley, *Jurists*, ch.1.

44 On the successors to the Roman jurists – their character, methodology and (lack of) connection to any given state apparatus, see the remainder of ibid.

45 For the methodology of the medieval Civilians, see James Gordley, 'Ius Quaerens Intellectum: The Method of the Medieval Civilians' in John W. Cairns and Paul J. du Plessis, *The Creation of the Ius Commune: From Casus to Regula* (EUP, 2010). For a useful account of 'the artificial divisions which modern academic methodologies can impose', see Leslie Dodd, *Thomas Craig's Aetiology of Law and Society: Literary Dependence and Independence in the Jus Feudale*, [2016] Journal of Legal History 121.

46 Hence Watson's refrain that 'the heroes of Continental law before codification are law professors': Watson, *Slave Law*, 4. It is interesting to note that this observation holds true of Scotland also, at least from the period of Union (when durable chairs of law at the universities came to be established – the teaching of law having been generally desired, but not consistently realised, at the Scottish universities) until the nineteenth century when (as enthusiastic beneficiaries of colonialism) 'the Scots came to view themselves increasingly as British': See Robin Evans-Jones and Helen Scott, 'Lord Atkin, *Donoghue v. Stevenson* and the *Lex Aquilia*: Civilian Roots of the "Neighbour" Principle' in Paul J. du Plessis (ed.), *Wrongful Damage to Property in Roman Law: British Perspectives* (EUP, 2018), at 258; Linda Colley, *Britons: Forging the Nation 1707–1837* (Yale University Press, 2009).

47 Hence – though a late example of the phenomenon – James Lorimer (a nineteenth-century Chair of the Law of Nature and Nations at Edinburgh University) stood as 'a hero of George Davie's' *Democratic Intellect* – see MacCormick, *Democratic Intellect*, at 174. One of the most significant of Lorimer's scholarly contributions, for present purposes, was his *Institutes of the Law of Nations* (Blackwood, 1884).

48 For the distinction between 'feudal law' and 'feudalism' proper, see Leslie Dodd, 'Historical Introduction' in Thomas Craig, *Jus Feudale Tribus Libris Comprehensum* (Stair Society, 2017), at xxix–xxx.

49 Consider, e.g., the Scottish Act Anent Slaughter of 1555 (APS ii 494, c.13) which opens by bemoaning the fact that 'the odious crimes of slaughter [is] daily committed within this realm': The Three Estates of the Parliament of Scotland did not lack the ability to legislate to denounce the killing of another as unlawful, even if they perhaps, at this time, lacked the political power to practically prevent these unlawful killings.

50 Watson, *Slave Law*, 2.

51 Ibid.

52 Ibid., at 2–3.

53 Note that while there is 'some evidence that Henry II was concerned with judicial administration', it seems he was not 'necessarily [concerned with] the content of substantive law': John Hudson, *The Formation of the English Common Law: Law and Society in England from King Alfred to Magna Carta* (2nd edn) (Routledge, 2018), at 138.

54 Watson, *Ambiguity*, 73–75.

55 I leave aside the political question of whether neglect may be benign.

56 Birks, 'More Logic', 174.

57 Gordley, *Jurists*, 27.

58 Of which, wee David M. Walker, *Legal Scholarship in Scotland* (1960) SLT (News) 10.

59 Reid, 'The Third Branch', 45.

60 Gretton, *Law Commissioning*, 145.

61 In this regard, the law commissioners may have more in common with the jurists of the later Dominate (or perhaps, more optimistically, with the jurists of Justinian's law commission in the sixth century) than with the classical jurists: Nonetheless, magnificent achievement though it was, the composition and positing of the *Corpus Iuris Civilis* did not mark 'the high water mark of Roman jurisprudence: that was reached by the great masters of the classical period, which had ended some three centuries before': James MacKintosh, *Roman Law in Modern Practice* (W. Green, 1934), at 53.

62 As Honoré observed, 'legal work done for the state, such as the drafting of Imperial constitutions [or, legislation more generally], does not appear to the classically-oriented mind as creative lawyerly work': Honoré, *Tribonian*, xiv.

63 Ibid., 140.

64 Birks was a staunch advocate for reducing incidences of confusion in the law, but clearly stood against viewing codification as a panacea for such: Birks, 'More Logic', at 168.

65 By Justinian's time, for instance, it was noted that 'the mere bulk of statute law was a serious obstacle to its application in practice' (MacKintosh, *Roman Law*, at 54). In the United Kingdom, it may be ventured that the preponderance of secondary legislation alone renders the law inaccessible to lawyers (of which, consider *R v. Chambers* [2008] EWCA Crim 2467) to say nothing of 'the man on the street'.

66 Birks, 'More Logic', 172.

67 Ibid., 173.

68 See Shona Wilson-Stark, *The Work of the British Law Commissions Law Reform ... Now?* (Hart, 2017), ch.2, III.

69 Ibid.

70 Both of which options were mooted, though the latter was certainly unpopular with the Scots: Ibid.

71 Gretton, *Law Commissioning*, at 123.

72 See Hector L. MacQueen, 'Glory with Gloag or the Stake with Stair? T B Smith and the Scots Law of Contract' in Reid and Carey Miller, *A Mixed Legal System in Transition*, at 157–166.

73 Harvey McGregor, *A Contract Code: Drawn Up on Behalf of the English Law Commission* (Giuffre Francis Lefebvre, 1993), at xxiii.

74 T.B. Smith, *Law Reform in a Mixed Civil Law and Common Law Jurisdiction*, (1975) Louisiana Law Review 927, at 947.

75 L.C.B. Gower, *Reflections on Law Reform*, (1973) University of Toronto Law Journal 257, 264–265.

76 Ibid., 264–265.

77 MacQueen, 'Glory', 157–166.

78 Ibid.

79 Gower, *Reflections*, 264–265.

80 Although the Scots institutional writers were natural lawyers to a man and indeed their works 'could only have been written on the basis of a natural law theory which authorises asserting as already law all principles conformable with "reason"' (see MacCormick, *Legal Reasoning*, 60), the modern Scot is typically so much a positivist (like the typically English lawyer) that it is difficult for them to conceptualise the mission of the institutional writers, who, they now (erroneously) conceptualise as having set forth a positive source of law in their treatises.

81 See, e.g., Megan Dewart, *The Scottish Legal System* (Bloomsbury, 2019), para.5.03.

82 For the foundational philosophical differences in the conception of law as articulated by a titan of Scots law and a titan of the English (Stair and Blackstone), see Alasdair MacIntyre, *Whose Justice? Which Rationality* (Duckworth, 1998), at 228–235.

83 Alexander McCall Smith, 'Scots Law in Comparative Context' in John P. Grant (ed.), *Independence and Devolution: The Legal Implications for Scotland* (W. Green, 1976), at 157.

84 Ibid., 159–160.

85 Scarman, *Law Commission*, 37.

86 Of course, as Smith points out, the Scots and English commissions each tend to mean something quite different when they used the term 'codification': Smith, *Law Reform*, 948.

87 See, generally, Robin Evans-Jones, *Receptions of Law, Mixed Legal Systems and the Myth of the Genius of Scots Private Law*, (1998) LQR 228; W. David H. Sellar, *Scots Law: Mixed from the Very Beginning? A Tale of Two Receptions*, (2000) Edin. L. R. 3.

88 Badouin Dupret and Gianluca Parolin, 'The Great Divide in Legal Discourse Towards a Global Historical Ontology of the Concept of Positive Law' in Badouin Dupret and Jean-Louis Halpérin, *State Law and Legal Positivism: The Global Rise of a New Paradigm* (Brill, 2021), 6.

89 Ibid.

90 See, too, François Dubois, 'Private Law in the Age of Rights' in Elspeth Reid and Daniel Visser, *Private Law and Human Rights: Bringing Rights Home in Scotland and South Africa* (EUP, 2013), 12.

91 Badouin Dupret, 'Introduction' in Dupret and Halpérin, *Legal Positivism*, 1.

92 Dupret and Parolin, 'Great Divide', 6.

93 For the links between the thought of Pufendorf, in particular, and Austin, see Watson, *Failures*, 120–125. Though it may be noted that Pufendorf was a natural lawyer rather than a positivist, 'natural law thinking having reached such a point as [his] it is but a short step to the outright positivism of a Bentham or the more qualified positivism of a John Austin': MacCormick, *Legal Reasoning*, 60.
94 Simpson, 'Legal Theory', at 80.
95 MacCormick, *Legal Reasoning*, 60.
96 It must be remembered that Justinian was not merely *primus inter pares* nor a constitutional guardian of the law, but *Dominus* – Lord – and despite the Christianisation of his Empire, a quasi-divine monarch: See Peter Sarris, *Justinian: Emperor, Soldier, Saint* (Basic Books, 2023), at 22.
97 MacKintosh, *Roman Law*, 55.
98 Craig Anderson, *Roman Law for Scots Law Students* (EUP, 2020), 61.
99 See Peter Birks and Grant MacLeod, 'Introduction' in *Justinian's Institutes* (Duckworth, 1987), 11.
100 Anderson, *Roman Law*, 63.
101 MacCormick, *Legal Reasoning*, 61.
102 MacKintosh, *Roman Law*, 53.
103 See, generally, Craig, *Jus Feudale*, 1.2.12.
104 MacKintosh, *Roman Law*, 54.
105 Ibid., 54.
106 See, generally, Alan Watson, *Legal Transplants: An Approach to Comparative Law* (2nd edn) (University of Georgia Press, 1993).
107 MacQueen, *Invincible*.
108 Martin Hogg, 'Codification of Private Law: Scots Law at the Crossroads of Common and Civil Law' in Barker, Fairweather and Grantham (eds), *Private Law in the 21st Century*, 107, 113.
109 Ibid.
110 Ibid.
111 Ian Ward, *English Legal Histories* (Bloomsbury, 2020), 338.
112 *Rex v. Inhabitants of Harberton* (1786) 1 Term Reports 139, 140.
113 Henry Home, *Lord Kames, Principles of Equity*, Volume 1 (3rd edn) (Bell and Creech, 1778), 20.
114 *Trade Fairs and Promotions (Pty) Ltd v. Thomson* 1984 4 SA 177 (W) 186–187, *per* Coetzee J.
115 See, generally, Jonathan Burchell, 'Personality Rights in South Africa: Re-affirming Dignity' in Niall R. Whitty and Reinhard Zimmermann, *Rights of Personality in Scots Law: A Comparative Perspective* (Dundee University Press, 2009), para.6.3.
116 Watson, *Society*, at xviii.
117 MacQueen, *Invincible*, 10.
118 The position of the SLC has, in fact, been complicated post-Devolution by the fact that, though the Commission retains 'the whole of the law of Scotland in its purview', the body is in fact funded by the Scottish government and 'the Scottish Government's budget is supposed to be used for devolved matters'. Thus, there has historically been some confusion as to the procedure for recommendations to be made by the Commission in respect of reserved matters: see Gretton, *Law Commissioning*, 130.
119 Hunter, *Law Reform*, 158, 163.
120 Hogg, 'Codification', at 114.

121 Watson, *Failures*, 36.
122 Stair, *Institutions*, 1, 1, 15.
123 MacQueen, *Invincible*, 10.
124 See Joe Thomson, *Northern Lights: Some Personal Reflections on Scottish Legal Scholarship* (2014) Jur. Rev. 83, at 93.
125 Scarman, *Law Commission*, 39.
126 Ibid., 37.
127 Ibid., 40.
128 Ibid.
129 MacQueen, *Invincible*, 10.
130 Ibid.
131 Ibid.
132 *Per* Gretton, at one time the convention was to appoint a judge of the Outer House, who was expected to step down if elevated to the Inner House: Gretton, *Law Commissioning*, 136. Lady Paton, however, was already an Inner House judge when appointed Chair of the SLC in 2019.
133 [2014] CSOH 76 [2017] A.C. 424.
134 Ibid., para.12.
135 See also *Akers and others v. Samba Financial Group* [2017] A.C. 424, at para.35, in which the UK Supreme Court approved of Lord Malcolm's Outer House judgement and so, also, the dual patrimony theory articulated in the discussion paper.
136 See Jonathan Brown, *Why Use Two Words When Just One Would Do? Some Thoughts on Section 15 of the Trusts and Succession (Scotland) Act 2024*, (2025) Edin. L. R. 302.
137 Stephen Cretney, *The Politics of Law Reform – A View from the Inside* (1985) MLR 493, 493.
138 Law Commissions Act 1965, s.2 (1).
139 Scarman, *Law Commission*, 33.
140 Burrows, *Obligations*, 2.
141 Scarman, *Law Commission*, 41.
142 Stair, *Institutions*, I, 1, 17.
143 See, generally, Laurent Jaffro, 'James Dalrymple, Viscount Stair, on Legal Normativity' in Alexander Broadie, *Scottish Philosophy in the Seventeenth Century* (OUP, 2020), 140–142.
144 Albeit practical, rather than pure reason – see the discussion in D. Neil MacCormick, *Practical Reason in Law and Morality* (OUP, 2008), *passim*.
145 See, generally, D. Neil MacCormick, *Rhetoric and the Rule of Law: A Theory of Legal Reasoning* (OUP, 2005).
146 Stair, *Institutions*, I, 1, 17.
147 Ibid.
148 Ibid.
149 Austin, *The Province of Jurisprudence Determined*.
150 Hans Kelsen, *Reine Rechtslehre* (1. Aufl, 1934).
151 H.L.A. Hart, *The Concept of Law* (Clarendon Press, 1961).
152 Like Kelsen and Hart, who *per* Simpson adopt 'weaker versions of positivism' than the crude and brute dogma advanced by Austin, positivists of whatever shade and conviction are united by the opinion that 'all law is positive law, and what this means at its simplest is that all laws owe their status as such to the fact that they have been laid down' – if not by a legislator *qua* legislator, then certainly by some 'power-conferring' rule, 'rule of competence' or 'rule of recognition': Simpson, 'Legal Theory', 80–83.

153 *Regula est, quae rem quae est breviter enarrat. non ex regula ius sumatur, sed ex iure quod est regula fiat. per regulam igitur brevis rerum narratio traditur, et, ut ait Sabinus, quasi causae coniectio est, quae simul cum in aliquo vitiata est, perdit officium suum*: D.50.17.1 (Paulus).

154 It is important to note that the term *ius* was initially 'taken to be something objectively right and discoverable, and in this sense it remained as a kind of synonym for "law" throughout the history of Latin as an effective language'. Further, it must be noted that for the Romans of the classical (and perhaps even Justinianic) period, *ius* denoted not a subjective 'right to' something, but rather – and exclusively – 'that which is [objectively] right': See Richard Tuck, *Natural Rights Theories: Their Origins and Development* (Cambridge University Press, 1979), at 8.

155 Latin: *casus*. That is not to say that justice was or is done in every case – merely that following the strictures of this approach, 'law' denotes those cases in which justice is done (i.e. in which the objectively 'right' decision is reached) and those cases in which the law is not applied (i.e. the 'wrong' decision is reached) are wrong and, being wrong, should not be taken to be representative of the law. This corresponds with George L. Gretton's 'Some Reflections' in Andrew J.M. Steven, Ross G. Anderson and John MacLeod, *Nothing so Practical as a Good Theory* (Avizandum, 2017), at 397.

156 *Iustitia est constans et perpetua voluntas ius suum cuique tribuens*: Justinian, *Institutes*, 1.1.*pr.*

157 See William M. Gordon, *Roman Law, Scots Law and Legal History: Selected Essays* (EUP, 2007), 317–318.

158 See Simpson, 'Legal Theory', 77.

159 Ibid.

160 John Austin, *Lectures*, Volume II (5th edn), at 655.

161 MacCormick, *Legal Reasoning*, 60.

162 In this sense, *lex* can be understood as a declaration of what the law is – which by its declared nature stands as 'both the only reason for saying that [x] is the law': See Simpson, 'Legal Theory', 86. Hence, an Act such as the Age of Legal Capacity (Scotland) Act 1991 is, here, a *lex* which provides a general rule (an authoritative and conclusive reason for holding) that a natural legal person must be over the age of 16 to enter into transactions.

163 Stair, *Institutions*, 1, 1, 16.

164 Stein, *Regulae Iuris*, 5.

165 Ibid., 1–33.

166 MacCormick, *Institutions of Law*, 11–14.

167 Lord Reid, a Scots judge who sat on the singular apex appellate court of Scotland and England, of course sought to blow apart this so-called 'fairy story' by letting the world know that there is in fact no 'Aladdin's cave' in which 'the common law in all its splendour' can be found (Lord Reid, *The Judge as Law-Maker*, (1972–73) 12 JSPTL 22, 22). Nonetheless, the view that law is – and may be – discovered rather than simply posited has rather more merit than his Lordship's pithy dismissal would appear to suggest.

168 Watson, *Ambiguity*, xi.

169 Ibid.

170 Such is not to say that non-judge jurists have not contributed to the development of the Common law – as Duxbury argued, 'the familiar argument that juristic speculation in England has been largely uninfluential as compared with similar pursuits elsewhere is often presented in an inordinately simplistic fashion. While the argument might be correct, its correctness is too often taken for granted':

Neil Duxbury, *Jurists and Judges* (Hart, 2001), at vii. The (simplistic) argument is not taken for granted here: rather, it is simply observed – drawing on the work of Watson and Paterson – that 'no club is so intellectually exclusive as English higher court judges' – and no elite so venerated within the English legal tradition: Watson, *Slave Law*, 5; Alan Paterson, *The Law Lords* (MacMillan Press, 1982), at 9–34. In Paterson's more recent study of the superior London-based judges, he again concluded that 'the most significant dialogues in relation to judicial decision-making in the final court are those which take place between its judges, and between judges and counsel, [though] other dialogues do have a[notably smaller] influence': see Alan Paterson, *Final Judgment: The Last Law Lords and the Supreme Court* (Hart, 2013), at 209–257.

171 Beginning in the nineteenth and into the twentieth centuries, certain – decidedly English – ideas which disavowed the utility of legal writing began to influence the Scottish courts. Consider the haughty dismissal of Professors Gretton and Reid by Lord Ross in *Deutz Engines Ltd. v. Terex Ltd.* 1984 SLT 273, at 275 – or worse still, consider the 'sneering abuse' that one Alan Rodger (later Lord Rodger of Earlsferry) was subjected to by Sheriff-Substitute Dickson in *Mercantile Credit Co Ltd v. Townsley* 1971 SLT (Sh Ct) 37 at 39. Nonetheless, textbooks and monographs continued to be used to significant effect in the Scots courts throughout this time period and down to the present day: Blackie and Whitty, 'Scotland', 79–81.

172 Outwith the Holy Roman Empire, which to some measure claimed continuity with the Roman state and so the law of Justinian, 'there was no theory that Justinian's *Corpus Iuris Civilis* had continued in force' in the jurisdictions of the European *ius commune* and – indeed, Scotland itself never formed a part of the Roman Empire. Watson, *Ambiguity*, 55. Though Roman law was referred to for its reason and equity, 'the problem of discovering what the Roman rule was had to be faced. (This leads on to the further difficult issue [...] of the authority of the interpretation of individual jurists [amongst other things])' (Watson, *Ambiguity*, at 56); crucially the point that is being made here is that the privilege of opining on 'that which is right' was not, in Scotland or the European Continent, limited to state-(or Crown)-appointed *iudices*, but the province of anyone who could justly claim to be 'learned in law'. Hence 'in the Eighteenth Century and before, advocates fortified their argument with copious citation from "the foreign doctors"': Smith, *Short Commentary*, 32.

173 Cf. the Roman jurists, who reasoned through the employment of a case-based methodology, but without the limitations of having to wait for a particular set of facts to crop up, and generate legal action, in the real world: Gordley, *Jurists*. 12.

174 Peter G. Stein, *Roman Law, Common Law and Civil Law*, [1992] Tulane Law Review 1591.

175 See Hudson, *Formation*, 15–17.

176 Stein, *Regulae Iuris*, 6–7.

177 Ibid., 19.

178 Consider the discussion in Ibid., 19–22, and compare this to the debate concerning whether or not the Appellate Committee of the House of Lords was to be regarded as bound by its own precedents in the nineteenth to twentieth centuries.

179 MacCormick, *Legal Reasoning*, 59.

180 Simpson, 'Legal Theory', 86.

181 Smith, *Law Reform*, 927, 945.

182 MacCormick, *Legal Reasoning*, 59.

183 Neither the Scots, nor the English, nor any other uncodified system 'admit[s] the possibility of a court, however elevated, reaching a final, authoritative statement of what the law is in a general abstract sense': Simpson, 'Legal Theory', 90.

184 Michelon, *The Authority of Doctrinal Scholarship.* The fact of a statute may stand by virtue of its own existence as a reason for proceeding in a certain way (Simpson, 'Legal Theory', 85) – but as is discussed below, in Scotland even a statute may not stand as a conclusively 'authoritative reason' in the sense described by Michelon.

185 Smith, *Short Commentary*, 34.

186 Provided, of course, that they can find some countervailing reason (such as distinctions of fact) to depart from past precedent.

187 Unlike in England, there has never been a separation of 'legal' and 'equitable' jurisdiction in Scotland and, indeed, the common law of Scotland and equity are taken by Stair to be harmonious with one another: Stair, *Institutions*, 1, 1, 16. The Court of Session and High Court of Justiciary are together styled 'the Supreme Courts of Scotland', despite the residence of the apex (civil) appellate court being in London, and the Court of Session is imbued with both an ordinary and extraordinary equitable jurisdiction.

188 Fallacy though it may be, no true Scotsman can resist the urge to point the reader to the infamous dicta of Lord Cooper in *MacCormick v. Lord Advocate* 1953 SC 396 here.

189 *M'Kenzie of Granville v. Stewart* (1752) Mor. 7443; *Roberts and His Curator Bonis, Petitioners* (1901) 3 F. 779. In each of these cases, 'the Court exercised its *nobile officium* to disapply a statutory provision because it regarded it as equitable to do so. The decision as applied to the facts of the case might not be substantively controversial, but the underlying principle is quite powerful': Stephen Thomson, *The Nobile Officium: The Extraordinary Equitable Jurisdiction of the Supreme Courts of Scotland* (Avizandum, 2015). See also Jamie McGowan, *The Nobile Officium and Public Law: An Undertapped Resource?* UKCLA March 12, 2024, https://ukconstitutionallaw.org/2024/03/12/jamie-mcgowan-the-nobile-officium-and-public-law-an-undertapped-resource/.

190 Watson, *Ambiguity*, 73–75.

191 To take but two arbitrary, but unquestionably uncontroversial, examples each reported at the turn of the last century, consider the cases of *Sharp v. Thomson* 1997 SC (HL) 66 and *McFarlane v. Tayside Health Board* 2000 S.C. (H.L) 1. In respect of the former, Gretton commented that the question 'what is the *ratio* of Sharp v. Thomson? [...] [is] as unanswerable as a Zen koan, but, unlike a koan, there was no bliss of enlightenment' (George L. Gretton, *Ownership and Insolvency Burnett's Tr v. Grainger*, (2004) Edin. L. R. 389, at 391), while Thomson's criticism of *McFarlane* saw the bench of the Appellate Committee of the House of Lords accused of 'abandoning the law of delict', and one judge in particular of 'not only abandon[ing] the law of delict, but law itself': Joe Thomson, *Abandoning the Law of Delict*, (2000) SLT (News) 43, at 44.

192 Lack of relevant technical knowledge, indifference to detail and the inherent difficulty of passing quality legislation, even in the absence of these first two factors, being chief among them.

193 Reid, 'The Third Branch'.

194 This was the purpose for which the series was designed *ab initio* and even a cursory review of reported Scots cases indicates that citation of SULI volumes is a staple of courts and tribunals at all levels in Scotland.

195 Consider *Gray v. Braid Logistics (UK) Ltd* [2017] CSOH 44: 'in this case, the court seems to have rather blindly followed English law [...] Judging from the case report

in *Gray* (although again, one cannot be sure on this point) [MacGregor's] *The Law of Agency in* Scotland was not cited to the court. Rather, the Outer House applied the English case, *The Borvigilant*'. See Laura J. MacGregor, *Agency Law in the Scottish Courts: Time for a Broader Approach?* (2019) Edin. L. R. 94, 99.

196 Gretton, *Law Commissioning*, 126.

197 Hogg, 'Codification', 114.

198 Roderick R.M. Paisley, *The Effect of Death in the Context of Succession* (Queen's University Belfast Seminar Paper, 10 March 2013), accessible at https://youtu.be/7EVDRsqxHcE?t=137.

199 Gretton, *Law Commissioning*, 126.

200 Lord Gill, *Quo Vadis Leges Romanorum?* (2019) SLG 53, 53; see also Jonathan Brown, *Scots Law as a Civilian System – A Response*, (2019) SLG 59, 60.

201 Ibid.

202 Brown, *Civilian System*, 60.

203 Ibid.

204 Law Commissions Act 1965, s.3 (1).

205 Birks, 'More Logic', 174.

206 Ibid.

207 See D.1.1.1 (Ulpian).

208 D.50.17.1 (Paulus).

209 Michelon, *The Authority of Doctrinal Scholarship.*

210 Ibid.

211 Simpson, 'Legal Theory', 85.

212 For the Institutional writers, as a closed class, may be able to lay claim to this ability also: see https://blogs.ed.ac.uk/private-law/2024/10/11/the-authority-of-doctrinal-scholarship/.

213 Birks, 'More Logic'.

214 See, broadly, James Drummond Young, Lord Drummond Young, *The Impetus for a New Moveable Transactions Law*, (2024) Jur. Rev. 200 and, more generally, that whole (special) volume of the *Juridical Review*.

CONCLUSION: MORE LOGIC AND LESS LEGISLATIVE FIAT

The commissioners of the SLC are expected to execute their office 'with a view to [the law's] systematic development and reform' including 'the reduction of separate enactments and generally the simplification and modernisation of the law'. This would appear to counsel against the proliferation of particular, bespoke, enactments. Nonetheless, the commissioners are also duty-bound to maintain a concern for the 'codification of such law'. Although a true codification in the European Continental style (whether under the Germanic, Napoleonic or some altogether different model) would unquestionably 'reduce the number of separate enactments' and, done well, undoubtedly 'eliminat[e] [...] anomalies [and] repeal obsolete and unnecessary enactments', thus discharging the law commissioners' statutory functions,[1] it is not merely the case that 'there is not much enthusiasm for codification' in this jurisdiction.[2] It remains the case, as Rahmatian observed, that 'the real problem for codification of Scots private law (apart from political issues) is whether Scottish legal culture is prepared fundamentally to change its approach to statutory interpretation'.[3] There is, at present, nothing to suggest that Scottish legal culture is so prepared and in fact one eminent judge recently considered that the very term 'codification' 'in some circles is regarded as a "forbidden" word'.[4]

Consequently, it would appear that the commissioners' duty to eventually bring about the holistic codification of Scots law must go unfulfilled for the foreseeable future. Where 'codification' is wrought in any of the UK's jurisdictions, it is merely a statutory quasi-codification in the form of, for example, the Partnership Act 1890, which is nonetheless subject to the ordinary rules of statutory interpretation.[5] This is obviously unsatisfactory and even enthusiastic advocates of codification, such as the first law commissioners, would caution that 'a patchwork quilt of improvements unrelated to the whole pattern of the law is apt to create as many problems as it solves'.[6] Nonetheless, as a more recent Scottish commissioner has observed, 'patchwork reform has replaced the ideal of comprehensive redevelopment'.[7] This is a regrettable state of affairs, but against the background of the ongoing supra-national 'positivisation of law' that has presently reached a high point, if not its final zenith, it can at least be rationally understood. Nonetheless, by tapping into the non-positivistic tradition of Scots law – by recognising the nature of 'law' as intimately connected with 'right' and 'reason', and by drawing on the historical willingness of the jurisdiction to consider non-legislative (or quasi-legislative) sources as 'reasons' to act in a certain way or believe certain things – the development of a 'systematic which [...] provides stability and a foundation for analysis and reflection without inhibiting improvement' can yet occur.[8]

To achieve this, it is 'Stair's intellectual spirit is what we chiefly need to encourage'.[9] That is not to say that we need to adopt his precise taxonomy and mode of organisation,[10] still less his theology.[11] It is, rather, his spirit of enquiry and drive to 'treat law as a rational discipline', and by extension to discern its precepts through reason and to organise them systematically, that must be encouraged. Apropos of this, it should be observed that whatever other flaws in organisation can be detected in Stair, the great jurist's philosophical taxonomy of 'obligations' – certainly of 'voluntary obligations' – remains, seemingly, sound today and continues to find favour in the courts of Scotland. Not only is Stair's separation of 'promise', as a separate species of unilaterally constituted *μονόπλευρος* obligation, from the (far more familiar) bilaterally constituted *διπλευρος* obligations arising *ex contractu* still observed in Scottish practice today, but indeed his rational explanation of the mode by which they are created (through acts of the will – particularly, and crucially, 'engagement') is in many ways far more satisfactory than the cruder 'offer + acceptance' analysis that has found favour in the past century.

Unlike in other systems of law, Scottish jurisprudents must seek to satisfactorily account for the place of unilaterally constituted 'promises' within the Scots legal order. 'Engagement' – signifying a juridical actor's *voluntas* [will] to be bound by an undertaking – not only ought to be, but seemingly has been taken, following Stair, to be the crucial factor for determining whether or not a voluntary obligation has been created in this jurisdiction. This has consequences for any attempt to reform the 'law of contract' in isolation: to do so will necessarily visit violence upon the coherence of the law. That this is the case can be seen by reference to the Contract (Rights of Third Parties) (Scotland) Act 2017, itself an SLC initiative concerning an area which the lead commissioner himself conceded might have been better left to the courts to reform. Prior to this Act's abolition of the Scots common law concept of *jus quaesitum tertio*, it was possible to explain the operation of this concept by reference to Stair's intellectual taxonomy: reciprocal acts of engagement between two or more parties could create a binding obligation, the beneficiary of which was extrinsic to the creation process. This phenomenon may well have been puzzling to Common – and even some Civilian – lawyers, schooled in lessons concerning the sanctity of so-called 'privity of contract'. To a Scot, following Stair, however, the situation is readily explicable; engagement, signifying will to be bound, can render one the debtor in an obligation, bound to pay or perform something to a creditor. If the creditor reciprocally engages – by 'accepting' an 'offer' of performance – then a contract will be created, but a contract is a separate species of voluntary obligation from 'promise' and, at common law, *ius quaesitum tertio.*

'Contracts', being mutual and *διπλευρος*, require reciprocal acts of engagement since both parties are bound to one another simultaneously as creditor-and-debtor. The exercise of *voluntas* being required to bind oneself to a debt (and being insufficient to bind anyone other than oneself to the necessity of performance) means that both parties must be seen, objectively, to wish to be bound by obligation. In contrast, where a 'promise' is concerned, the singular act of engagement of the prospective obligant suffices, because the resultant obligation being *μονόπλευρος* (binding the promissor to the necessity of performance only), only the promissor is bound, as debtor, to perform within terms of the obligation. *Mutatis mutandis*, this is true of the common law *ius quaesitum tertio.* It, on this analysis, appears to give rise to a bilaterally constituted, but ultimately *μονόπλευρος*, obligation. Like a promise, the beneficiary of the *ius quaesitum tertio* need not accept, or even know of, the existence of the *ius* for it to bind its creators to the necessity of performance: the *ius quaesitum tertio* is created by the expressed will of the parties to the contract, but it is not merely a part of the contract itself. Hence, the fact that the obligation (itself a *res* or thing) arising out of the contract cannot, following its creation, be altered or revoked by the contracting parties, is readily explicable: the *ius quaesitum tertio* is a separate obligation from the contract itself; although created bilaterally, the *ius quaesitum tertio* is *μονόπλευρος*, while the bilaterally constituted contract is, in contrast, both mutual and *διπλευρος*.

The 2017 Act abolished the common law concept of *ius quaesitum tertio* and replaced it with a framework which positively mandates the recognition of enforceable 'third party rights' only when certain statutory conditions are met. As previously, it is the case that two or more persons can agree to confer a benefit upon a third party and that third party can thereafter enforce that agreement so as to seek 'as a remedy for breach of the undertaking, any remedy for breach which a contracting party would be entitled to were the undertaking one in favour of the contracting party'.[12] Now, however, the agreement to confer a third-party right upon another cannot satisfactorily be analysed in accordance with Stair's typology; rather than the reciprocal acts of engagement, on the parts of the respective obligants, creating an enforceable undertaking binding as a result of their will, now – *per* s.3 (1) of the Act – the 'undertaking contained in a contract which has given rise to a third-party right may be cancelled or modified by the contracting parties'. It will only be in certain, prescribed, circumstances that the third-party right will stand fixed, unalterable and *ipso facto* enforceable; none of these circumstances turn on the will or intention of the debtors in the relevant obligation, but rather turn on the creditor in that obligation being made somehow aware of their right to seek performance of the undertaking.[13]

This, more than perhaps was realised at the time of the 2017 Act's passing, critically undermines the coherence of the Scots law of voluntary obligations, and so the broader framework of obligations and private law as an ordered, rational subject of study. Legislation, of course, 'can break entirely with the existing tradition',[14] but that something 'can' is an entirely different matter from whether or not it should. In having a tradition of rational overview literature, Scots lawyers might – as Birks suggested – stand justifiably proud. There is a lot to commend the flexibility of a system which – though unconstrained by codification – is nonetheless structurally ordered and principled rather than in the position of the altogether more chaotic Anglo-American Common law. The advantages conferred by the Scots tradition were, however, being 'frittered away' at the time of Birks' writing and at this stage of the twenty-first century, altogether more worryingly, are being actively thrown away – not by the bogeyman of an Anglicising legislature based in London, but rather by a legislative body based in the heart of Edinburgh itself, aided by a body of august and eminent Scots lawyers.

The state of affairs that has developed hitherto is unfortunate, but alas the assault on the underlying rational principles of Scots law continues. If the proposed Contract (Formation) (Scotland) Bill passes into law, then the most readily recognised, and certainly most commonly litigated, species of voluntary obligation will be taken out of the rational legal framework which developed at common law and will rest instead entirely on the posited authority of the legislature. This, it might be feared, will leave the law pertaining to unilaterally constituted promise to atrophy, but more than this it will mean that there is no systematised framework of 'voluntary obligations' – that is, legal bonds created by 'acts of the will' – in Scotland anymore. Scotland would, thus, be seen to be throwing away one of its most significant assets – indeed, perhaps, throwing away the very reason that Scots law has continued to subsist for three centuries within a Union, Empire and Commonwealth fundamentally dominated by Common lawyers and Common law thinking.

Stair's taxonomy of *ex voluntate* obligations was and is, to again use Bell's words, 'so well digested in all its parts, so liberal in principle, so good in arrangement, so distinguished for sound judgment and excellent adaptation to the business and concerns of men that it would seem almost beyond the age in which it was written'.[15] That this is so can be evidenced by reference to the fact that the so-called 'postal acceptance rule' – erroneously conceptualised as a mere English oddity received unbidden into our law – is in fact little more than a generic instance of the application of the consequences of Stair's *explananda* which could readily be extended to novel technological developments such as mobile phones and emails. Indeed, it should perhaps be borne in mind that for Stair himself the post office would have been seen as something of an innovation; Scotland's pre-union General Post Office was established following an Act of 1695, some two years after the publication of the second edition of his *Institutions*.[16] This notwithstanding, Bell – writing well over a century later than Stair – was able to plainly state that 'it is the act of acceptance that binds the bargain; and in the common case it is not necessary that the acceptance shall have reached the person who makes the offer'.[17]

The significance of an 'act' – rather than communication – is consistent with a law of voluntary obligations; that is, a law in which legal bonds are created by acts of the will, rather than exchanges underpinned by formalities of whatever measure. Though the respondents to the SLC discussion paper on voluntary obligations may not mourn the passing of the 'postal acceptance rule', if such is brought about, it is here thought that there would in fact be much lost if legislation of the kind proposed by the SLC is passed. Consequently, as stated at the outset of this short book, the argument here is one of 'anti-law reform advocacy': whatever problems there may be with the present law, plainly positing a novel Act, which pays no heed to the intricacies of the Scottish legal tradition and inheritance, would introduce more uncertainty, undermine the overarching coherence of our jurisprudence and ultimately render the law far more unsatisfactory than it is now. Quasi-codification, if brought to bear in this area without due accord paid to the broader legal framework, would at a stroke shatter the structure of the law while at the same time impeding subsequent innovation and criticism.[18]

Such is not to say that 'law reform' is never warranted; the law would indeed stagnate if there were not jurists such as those in the SLC prepared to do the often unglamorous 'technical' work involved in ensuring that it is able to meet the needs of an evolving society. The unglamorous work of law reform is, however, sometimes best carried out in an unglamorous way – not every house requires the 'éclat of a new extension'[19] and indeed, a building onto which innumerable additions have been grafted on is more likely to appear ramshackle and unsightly than it is to in fact stand as a satisfactory construction. Consequently, as the title of this chapter might be taken to suggest, it is suggested here that the best way forward – the way that will allow for the Scottish legal system to develop most satisfactorily (as it did for centuries) – is for the SLC to privilege the application of legal logic in the composition of its reports, over urging Parliament to solve perceived problems by legislative fiat. The law pertaining to voluntary obligations – particularly the formation of voluntary obligations – in Scotland is capable of rational development through the intellectual efforts of courts and jurists. Thus, it should be allowed to do so.

Notes

1 Each of the quotations in this paragraph hitherto has been drawn from s.3 (1) of the 1965 Act.
2 Gretton, *Law Commissioning*, 132.
3 Andreas Rahmatian, *Codification of Private Law in Scotland: Observations by a Civil Lawyer* (2017) Oxford U Comparative L Forum 1, at ouclf.law.ox.ac.uk, at fn.78.
4 Drummond-Young, *Impetus*, at 201.
5 https://blogs.ed.ac.uk/private-law/2024/10/11/the-authority-of-doctrinal-scholarship/.
6 Scarman, *Law Commission*, 33.
7 Gretton, *Law Commissioning*, 126.
8 Birks, 'More Logic', 173.
9 Ibid.
10 'Stair made major modifications of the institutional system, most of which, it has to be said, either did not take root or, having taken root, have not in the end proved very helpful': Birks, 'Definition and Division', 28.
11 Stair would likely be horrified that the latest Scottish census revealed over half of the populace to be either irreligious or atheistic: see https://www.scotlandscensus.gov.uk/2022-results/scotland-s-census-2022-ethnic-group-national-identity-language-and-religion/.
12 Contract (Third Party Rights) (Scotland) Act 2017, s.7(2).
13 Ibid., ss.4–6.
14 Watson, *Failures*, 36.
15 Bell, *Commentaries*, ix.
16 An Act Anent the Post Office 1695 APS ix 417, c.31.
17 Bell, *Commentaries*, at 326–327.
18 Birks, 'More Logic', 173.
19 Gretton, *Law Commissioning*, 127.

BIBLIOGRAPHY

Articles

Adelyn Wilson, *Stair and the Inleydinge of Grotius*, [2010] Edin. L. R. 259.

Adrian D. Ward and Polona Curk, *Respecting 'Will': Viscount Stair and Online Shopping*, [2018] SLT (News) 123.

Alan Rodger, Lord Rodger of Earlsferry, *Only Connect*, [2007] Jur. Rev. 164.

Andreas Rahmatian, *The Role of Institutional Writers in Scots Law*, [2018] Jur. Rev. 42, at 44.

D. Neil MacCormick, *The Democratic Intellect and the Law*, [1985] Legal Studies 172.

David M. Walker, *Legal Scholarship in Scotland*, (1960) SLT (News) 10.

Douglas Brodie, *Pursuing the Police and Assumption of Responsibility: Tindall v Chief Constable of Thames Valley*, [2022] Jur. Rev. 100, at 104.

Eric Descheemaeker, *Mapping the Common Law: On a Recent English Attempt and its Links with Scottish Jurisprudence*, [2003] Jur. Rev. 295.

George L. Gretton, *Legal Science or Law Lite?* [2006] JLSS 44, at 44.

George L. Gretton, *Missives by Fax or Pdf?* [2010] Edin. L. R. 280.

George L. Gretton, *On Law Commissioning*, [2013] Edin. L. R. 119.

George L. Gretton, *Ownership and Insolvency Burnett's Tr v Grainger*, (2004) Edin. L. R. 389.

Hector L. MacQueen, *Invincible or Just a Flesh-Wound: The Holy Grail of Scots Law*, (2014) Legal Information Management 2, at 10.

Hector L. MacQueen, *My Word is My Bond: Unilateral Promises Once More*, [2019] SLT (News) 103.

Hector L. MacQueen, *Unilateral Undertakings*, [1986] SLT (News) 1.

J.J. Gow, *The Constitution and Proof of Voluntary Obligations: Part I*, [1961] Jur. Rev. 1.

James Drummond-Young, Lord Drummond Young, *The Impetus for a New Moveable Transactions Law*, (2024) Jur. Rev. 200.

Joe Thomson, *Abandoning the Law of Delict*, (2000) SLT (News) 43.

Joe Thomson, *Northern Lights: Some Personal Reflections on Scottish Legal Scholarship*, (2014) Jur. Rev. 83, at 93.

Joe Thomson, *Promises and the Requirements of Writing*, [1997] SLT (News) 284.

John W.G. Blackie, *Loss in the Post: Uncertainty of the Law*, [1974] JLSS 134.

Jonathan Brown, *Jus Quaesitum Tertio: A Res, Not A Right?* [2017] Jur. Rev. 53.

Jonathan Brown, *Medical Intervention and Incapax Patients: The Place of Negotiorum Gestio within Law's 'Fundamental Structural Language'*, [2022] Edin. L. R. 422, at 422.

Jonathan Brown, *On Promises, Partnership and Succession*, [2023] Jur. Rev. 121.

Jonathan Brown, *Scots Law as a Civilian System – A Response*, (2019) SLG 59, at 60.

Jonathan Brown, *Why Use Two Words When Just One Would Do? Some Thoughts on Section 15 of the Trusts and Succession (Scotland) Act 2024*, (2025) Edin. L. R. 302.

Kenneth G.C. Reid, *From Text-Book to Book of Authority: The Principles of George Joseph Bell*, [2011] Edin. L. R. 6, at 6.
L.C.B. Gower, *Reflections on Law Reform*, (1973) University of Toronto Law Journal 257.
Laura J. MacGregor, *Agency Law in the Scottish Courts: Time for a Broader Approach?* (2019) Edin. L. R. 94.
Leslie Dodd, *Thomas Craig's Aetiology of Law and Society: Literary Dependence and Independence in the Jus Feudale*, [2016] Journal of Legal History 121.
Leslie Scarman, *The Law Commission*, (1972) Anglo-American Law Review 31.
Lord Gill, *Quo Vadis Leges Romanorum?* (2019) SLG 53, at 53.
Lord Hunter, *Law Reform: The Scottish Law Commission*, [1988] Jur. Rev. 158 at 163.
Lord Hunter, *Thomas Broun Smith 1915–1988*, [1992] Proceedings of the British Academy 455.
Lord Reid, *The Judge as Law-Maker*, (1972–73) 12 JSPTL 22, at 22.
Martin Hogg, *A Few Tricky Problems Surrounding Unilateral Promises*, [1997] SLT (News) 25.
Martin Hogg, *Contract Formation in the Electronic Age*, [2009] Edin. L. R. 121, at 125.
Martin Hogg, *Perspectives on Contract Theory from a Mixed Jurisdiction*, [2009] OJLS 643.
Martin Hogg, *Promise: The Neglected Obligation in European Private Law*, [2010] International and Comparative Law Quarterly 461.
Nick Sage, *The Significance of Adams v Lindsell*, [2020] JCL 179.
Nikolaos A. Davrados, R*estating the Civil Law of Quasi-Contract: Negotiorum Gestio and Unjust Enrichment*, [2023] J. Civil L. Stud. 1, at 3.
Peter G. Stein, *Roman Law, Common Law and Civil Law*, [1992] Tulane Law Review 1591.
Robin Evans-Jones, *Receptions of Law, Mixed Legal Systems and the Myth of the Genius of Scots Private Law*, (1998) LQR 228.
Shivprasad Swaminathan, *The Will Theorist's Mailbox: Misunderstanding the Moment of Contract Formation in the Indian Contract Act 1872*, [2018] Statute Law Review 14.
Shona Wilson-Stark, *The Longer You Can Look Back, The Further You Can Look Forward: The Origins of the Scottish Law Commission*, [2014] Edin. L. R. 59.
Stephen Bogle and Bobby Lindsay, *How Serious is the Serious Harm Threshold*? (SSRN, Working draft - 22/3/24).
Stephen Cretney, *The Politics of Law Reform – A View from the Inside*, (1985) MLR 4963.
Stephen Thomson, *Mixed Jurisdiction and the Scottish Legal Tradition: Reconsidering the Concept of Mixture*, [2014] J. Civ. L. Stud. 7.
T.B. Smith, *Law Reform in a Mixed Civil Law and Common Law Jurisdiction*, (1975) Louisiana Law Review 927.
W. David H. Sellar, *Scots Law: Mixed from the Very Beginning? A Tale of Two Receptions*, (2000) Edin. L. R. 3.
William W. McBryde, *Promises in Scots Law*, [1993] ICLQ 48, at 56.

Books

Alan Paterson, *Final Judgment: The Last Law Lords and the Supreme Court* (Hart, 2013).
Alan Paterson, *The Law Lords* (MacMillan Press, 1982).
Alan Watson, *Failures of the Legal Imagination* (University of Pennsylvania Press, 1988).
Alan Watson, *Legal Transplants: An Approach to Comparative Law* (2nd edn) (University of Georgia Press, 1993).
Alan Watson, *Slave Law in the Americas* (The University of Georgia Press, 1989).

Alan Watson, *Society and Legal Change* (2nd edn) (Temple University Press, 2001).
Alan Watson, *Sources of Law, Legal Change and Ambiguity* (T&T Clark Ltd., 1985), at 52.
Alasdair MacIntyre, *Whose Justice? Which Rationality* (Duckworth, 1998).
Andrew Burrows, *Understanding the Law of Obligations: Essays on Contract, Tort and Restitution* (Hart Publishing, 1998).
Bankton, *Institute of the Law of Scotland*, Volume 1 (Fleming, 1751).
Bell, *Principles of the Law of Scotland* (2nd edn) (Blackwood, 1830).
Craig Anderson, *Roman Law for Scots Law Students* (EUP, 2020), at 61.

D. Neil MacCormick, *Institutions of Law* (Oxford University Press, 2007).
D. Neil MacCormick, *Legal Reasoning and Legal Theory* (Clarendon, 1978).
D. Neil MacCormick, *Practical Reason in Law and Morality* (Oxford University Press, 2008).
D. Neil MacCormick, *Rhetoric and the Rule of Law: A Theory of Legal Reasoning* (Oxford University Press, 2005).
David M. Walker, *The Law of Contracts and Related Obligations in Scotland* (3rd edn) (T&T Clark, 1995).
Elspeth C. Reid and John W.G. Blackie, *Personal Bar* (W. Green, 2006).
George E. Davie, *The Crisis of the Democratic Intellect* (Polygon, 1986).
George E. Davie, *The Democratic Intellect: Scotland and Her Universities in the Nineteenth Century* (Edinburgh University Press, 1961).
George Joseph Bell, *Commentaries on the Laws of Scotland and on the Principles of Mercantile Jurisprudence*, Volume I (5th edn) (Blackwood, 1826).
Gillian Black, *Woolman and Black on Contract* (W. Green, 2018).
H.L.A. Hart, *The Concept of Law* (Clarendon Press, 1961).
Hans Kelsen, *Reine Rechtslehre* (1. Aufl, 1934).
Harvey McGregor, *A Contract Code: Drawn up on Behalf of the English Law Commission* (Giuffre Francis Lefebvre, 1993).
Hector L. MacQueen, *MacQueen and Thomson on Contract Law in Scotland* (6th edn) (Bloomsbury Professional, 2024).
Henry Cockburn, *Circuit Journeys* (Edinburgh: David Douglas, 1888), at 203.
Henry Home, *Lord Kames' Principles of Equity* (5th edn) (Bell and Bradfute, 1825).
Hugh Beale (ed.), *Chitty on Contracts* (35th edn) Volume 1 (Sweet and Maxwell, 2023), para.4.011.
Ian Ward, *English Legal Histories* (Bloomsbury, 2020), at 338.
James Gordley, *The Jurists: A Critical History* (Oxford University Press, 2013).
James Gordley, *The Philosophical Origins of Modern Contract Doctrine* (Clarendon Press, 1991).
James Lorimer, *Institutes of the Law of Nations* (Blackwood, 1884).
James MacKintosh, *Roman Law in Modern Practice* (W. Green, 1934).
Joe Thomson, *Scots Private Law* (W. Green, 2006).
John Austin, *Lectures*, Volume II (5th edn) (John Murray, 1885).
John Austin, *Province of Jurisprudence Determined* (John Murray, 1832).
John Ford, *Law and Opinion in Scotland During the Seventeenth Century* (Hart, 2007).
John Hudson, *The Formation of the English Common Law: Law and Society in England from King Alfred to Magna Carta* (2nd edn) (Routledge, 2018).
John J. Powell, *An Essay Upon the Law of Contracts and Agreements* (Chamberlaine et al., 1790).
Linda Colley, *Britons: Forging the Nation 1707–1837* (Yale University Press, 2009).
Martin Hogg, *Obligations* (2nd edn) (Avizandum, 2006).
Martin Hogg, *Obligations: Law and Language* (Cambridge University Press, 2017).

Megan Dewart, *The Scottish Legal System* (Bloomsbury, 2019).
Neil Duxbury, *Jurists and Judges* (Hart, 2001).
Peter Sarris, *Justinian: Emperor, Soldier, Saint* (Basic Books, 2023), at 22.
Peter Stein, *Regulae Iuris: From Juristic Rules to Legal Maxims* (Edinburgh University Press, 1966).
Reinhard Zimmermann, *The Law of Obligations: Roman Foundations of the Civilian Tradition* (Oxford University Press, 1990).
Richard Tuck, *Natural Rights Theories: Their Origins and Development* (Cambridge University Press, 1979).
Robert J. Pothier, *Traité des Obligations* (Chez Rouzeau-Montaut, 1761), translated into English by François X. Martin, *A Treatise on Obligations: Considered in a Moral and Legal View* (Martin and Ogden, 1802).
Shona Wilson-Stark, *The Work of the British Law Commissions Law Reform... Now?* (Hart, 2017).
Sir Frederick Pollock and Frederic W. Maitland, *The History of English Law Before the Time of Edward I* (2nd edn) (Cambridge University Press, 1898), at 184.
Stair, *Institutions of the Law of Scotland* (Andrew Anderson, 1681; 2nd edn, 1693).
Stair Memorial Encyclopaedia, *Obligations*, Volume 15.
Stephen Bogle, *Contract Before the Enlightenment: The Ideas of James Dalrymple, Viscount Stair, 1619–1695* (Oxford University Press, 2023), at 71.
Stephen Thomson, *The Nobile Officium: The Extraordinary Equitable Jurisdiction of the Supreme Courts of Scotland* (Avizandum, 2015).
T.B. Smith, *Short Commentary on the Law of Scotland* (W. Green, 1962).
Thesaurus Juris Civilis (H. W. Meyer, 1717).
Tony Honoré, *Tribonian* (Bloomsbury, 1978).
Vernon V. Palmer (ed.), *Mixed Jurisdictions Worldwide* (2nd edn) (Cambridge University Press, 2012).
William M. Gordon, *Roman Law, Scots Law and Legal History: Selected Essays* (EUP, 2007), at 317–318.
William M. Gloag, *The Law of Contract: A Treatise on the Principles of Contract in the Law of Scotland* (2nd edn) (Caledonian Books, 1985).
William W. McBryde, *Contract Law in Scotland* (3rd edn) (W. Green, 2007).

Book Chapters

A.W.B. Simpson, 'The Common Law and Legal Theory' in Simpson (ed.), *Oxford Essays in Jurisprudence: Second Series* (Clarendon Press, 1973), at 80.
Alexander McCall Smith, 'Scots Law in Comparative Context' in John P. Grant (ed.), *Independence and Devolution: The Legal Implications for Scotland* (W. Green, 1976).
Antoine Berman, 'La traduction et la lettre – ou l'auberge du lointain' in Antoine Berman (ed.), *Les Tours de Babel: Essais sur la Traduction* (Mauzevin, 1985).
Arthur T. Von Mehren, Hao Jiang and James R. Gordley, *An Introduction to the Comparative Study of Private Law: Readings, Cases, Materials* (2nd edn) (Cambridge University Press, 2021), at 3.
Badouin Dupret, 'Introduction' in Badouin Dupret and Jean-Louis Halpérin, *State Law and Legal Positivism: The Global Rise of a New Paradigm* (Brill, 2021), at 1.

Badouin Dupret and Gianluca Parolin, 'The Great Divide in Legal Discourse Towards a Global Historical Ontology of the Concept of Positive Law' in Badouin Dupret and Jean-Louis Halpérin, *State Law and Legal Positivism: The Global Rise of a New Paradigm* (Brill, 2021), at 6.

Brian Pillans, 'Delictual Liability at Common Law' in Joe Thomson (ed.), *Delict* (W. Green, 2007).

Eric Clive, 'Nothing So Practical as a Good Theory: The Notion of a Requirement' in Andrew J.M. Steven, Ross G. Anderson and John MacLeod, *Nothing So Practical as a Good Theory: Festschrift for George L. Gretton* (Avizandum, 2017).

François Dubois, 'Private Law in the Age of Rights' in Elspeth Reid and Daniel Visser, *Private Law and Human Rights: Bringing Rights Home in Scotland and South Africa* (Edinburgh University Press, 2013).

G. Campbell H. Paton, 'Comparison Between the Institutions and Other Institutional Writings' in David M. Walker (ed.), *Stair Tercentenary Studies* (Stair Society, 1981).

George L. Gretton, 'Some Reflections' in Andrew J.M. Steven, Ross G. Anderson and John MacLeod, *Nothing so Practical as a Good Theory* (Avizandum, 2017), at 397.

George L. Gretton, 'The Rational and the National: Thomas Broun Smith' in Elspeth C. Reid and David L. Carey Miller, *A Mixed Legal System in Transition: T. B. Smith and the Progress of Scots Law* (Edinburgh University Press, 2005), at 33.

Gerhard Lubbe, 'Formation of Contract' in Kenneth Reid and Reinhard Zimmermann, *A History of Private Law in Scotland: Volume 2: Obligations* (Oxford University Press, 2000).

Gordon M. Hutton, 'Purposes and Pattern of the Institutions: Stair's Aim in Writing the Institutions' in David M. Walker (ed.), *Stair Tercentenary Studies* (The Stair Society, 1981).

Hector L. MacQueen, 'A Post-Positivist Outlook from the Thistle' in Neil Walker (ed.), *MacCormick's Scotland* (Edinburgh University Press, 2012).

Hector L. MacQueen, 'Glory with Gloag or the Stake with Stair? T B Smith and the Scots Law of Contract' in Elspeth C. Reid and David L. Carey Miller, *A Mixed Legal System in Transition: T. B. Smith and the Progress of Scots Law* (Edinburgh University Press, 2005).

Hector L. MacQueen, 'Its in the Post! Distance Contracting in Scotland 1681–1855' in Frankie MacCarthy, James Chalmers and Stephen Bogle (eds), *Essays in Conveyancing and Property Law in Honour of Professor Robert Rennie* (Open Book Publishers, 2015).

Hector L. MacQueen, 'The Law of Obligations in Scots Law' in Reiner Schulze and Fryderyk Zoll (eds), *The Law of Obligations in Europe: A New Wave of Codifications* (Sellier European Law Publishers, 2013).

Howell A. Llyod (trs.), 'Introduction' in *François Hotman: Antitribonian* (Brill, 2021).

James G. Kellas, 'Lawyers in Contemporary Scottish Politics: A New "Dundas Despotism"?' in Lindsay Farmer and Scott Veitch (eds), *The State of Scots Law* (Butterworth, 2001).

James Gordley, '*Ius Quaerens Intellectum*: The Method of the Medieval Civilians', in John W. Cairns and Paul J. du Plessis, *The Creation of the Ius Commune: From Casus to Regula* (Edinburgh University Press, 2010).

John Cairns, 'Institutional Writings in Scotland Reconsidered' in Albert Kiralfy and Hector L. MacQueen (eds), *New Perspectives in Scottish Legal History* (Frank Cass, 1984).

John W.G. Blackie, 'Stair's Later Reputation as a Jurist' in David M. Walker (ed.), *Stair Tercentenary Studies* (Stair Society, 1981), at 227.

John W.G. Blackie and Niall R. Whitty, 'Scotland and the New Ius Commune' in Hector L. MacQueen (ed.), *Scots Law into the 21st Century: Essays in Honour of W. A. Wilson* (W. Green, 1996), at 79–81.

Jonathan Burchell, 'Personality Rights in South Africa: Re-affirming Dignity' in Niall R. Whitty and Reinhard Zimmermann, *Rights of Personality in Scots Law: A Comparative Perspective* (Dundee University Press, 2009).

Kenneth G.C. Reid, 'The Third Branch of the Profession: The Rise of the Academic Lawyer in Scotland' in Hector L. MacQueen (ed.), *Scots Law into the 21st Century: Essays in Honour of W. A. Wilson* (W. Green, 1996).

Laura MacGregor, 'Introduction' in George Joseph Bell, *Commentaries on the Laws of Scotland and on the Principles of Mercantile Jurisprudence*, Volume I (Edinburgh Legal Education Trust, 2023).

Laurent Jaffro, 'James Dalrymple, Viscount Stair, on Legal Normativity' in Alexander Broadie, *Scottish Philosophy in the Seventeenth Century* (Oxford University Press, 2020), at 140–142.

Leslie Dodd, 'Historical Introduction' in Thomas Craig, *Jus Feudale Tribus Libris Comprehensum*, Volume I (Stair Society, 2017), at xxix–xxx.

Leslie Dodd, 'Introduction' in *Jus Feudale Tribus Libris Comprehensum*, Volume II (Stair Society, 2025).

Lionel Smith, 'Stateless Trusts', in Lionel Smith (ed.), *The Worlds of the Trust* (Cambridge University Press, 2013), 96.

Martin Hogg, 'Codification of Private Law: Scots Law at the Crossroads of Common and Civil Law' in Kit Barker, Karen Fairweather and Ross Grantham (eds), *Private Law in the 21st Century* (Hart, 2017), 107.

Peter Birks, 'Definition and Division: A Meditation on Institutes 3.13' in Peter Birks (ed.), *The Classification of Obligations* (Clarendon Press, 1997).

Peter Birks, 'More Logic and Less Experience: The Difference Between Scots and English Law' in David L. Carey Miller and Reinhard Zimmermann, *The Civilian Tradition and Scots Law: Aberdeen Quincentenary Essays* (Duncker and Humblot, 1997).

Peter Birks and Grant MacLeod, 'Introduction' in *Justinian's Institutes* (Duckworth, 1987).

Phillip H. Brodie (Lord Brodie), 'From Scotland and Ireland' in Louis Blom-Cooper, Brice Dickson and Gavin Drewry (eds), *The Judicial House of Lords 1876 – 2009* (Oxford University Press, 2009), at 289.

Robin Evans-Jones and Helen Scott, 'Lord Atkin, Donoghue v Stevenson and the Lex Aquilia: Civilian Roots of the 'Neighbour' Principle' in Paul J. du Plessis (ed.), *Wrongful Damage to Property in Roman Law: British Perspectives* (Edinburgh University Press, 2018).

Ross G. Anderson, 'Introduction' in George Watson (ed.), *Bell's Dictionary and Digest of the Law of Scotland* (Edinburgh Legal Education Trust, 2012).

Vernon V. Palmer, 'Contracts of Intellectual Gratification – a Louisiana-Scotland Creation', in Vernon V. Palmer and Elspeth C. Reid, *Mixed Jurisdictions Compared: Private Law in Louisiana and Scotland* (Edinburgh University Press, 2009), at 217.

W.A. Wilson, 'Roman Quasi-Delicts and Scots Law' in *Roman Law, Scots Law and Legal History: Selected Essays* (Edinburgh University Press, 2007).

W. David H. Sellar, 'Promise' in Kenneth Reid and Reinhard Zimmermann, *A History of Private Law in Scotland: Volume 2: Obligations* (Oxford University Press, 2000).

Blogs

Andreas Rahmatian, *Codification of Private Law in Scotland: Observations by a Civil Lawyer,* (2017) Oxford U Comparative L Forum 1 at ouclf.law.ox.ac.uk.

Claudio Michelon, *The Authority of Doctrinal Scholarship*, [2024] Edinburgh Private Law Blog, accessible at https://blogs.ed.ac.uk/private-law/2024/10/11/the-authority-of-doctrinal-scholarship/.

Douglas Mathie, *Third-party Rights – Scots Law Stuck in the 17 Century*, August 2010, accessible at https://brodiestechblog.wordpress.com/2010/08/26/third-party-rights-%E2%80%93-scots-law-stuck-in-the17thcentury/.

Jamie McGowan, *The Nobile Officium and Public Law: An Undertapped Resource?* UKCLA 12 March 2024, https://ukconstitutionallaw.org/2024/03/12/jamie-mcgowan-the-nobile-officium-and-public-law-an-undertapped-resource/.

John Paul Sheridan, *Contract Law in Flux*, [2018] JLSS, accessible at https://www.lawscot.org.uk/members/journal/issues/vol-63-issue-01/contract-law-in-flux/.

Niall R. Whitty, *Unjustified Enrichment in Scots Law: Time for Consolidation, not Reappraisal?* [2022] Edinburgh Private Law Blog, accessible at https://blogs.ed.ac.uk/private-law/2022/05/05/unjustified-enrichment-in-scots-law-time-for-consolidation-not-reappraisal/.

Shepherd & Wedderburn, 'Goodbye "Postal Acceptance Rule", Hello "Out-of-Office Message" Rule?' 05 September 2017, at https://goo.gl/5evhjK.

Hansard

HC Debate 8 February 1965 col 55.

HL Debate 1 April 1965, col 1156.

PhD Theses

Adelyn L.M. Wilson, *The Sources and Method of the Institutions of the Law of Scotland by Sir James Dalrymple, 1st Viscount Stair, with Specific Reference to the Law of Obligations*, [2011] PhD Thesis, University of Edinburgh, at 15.

Reports and Discussion Papers

Contract (Formation) (Scotland) Bill Informal Consultation on Working Draft – 1 September to 3 November 2017.

Justice Directorate, *Scottish Law Commission – Contract Law Review Report: Consultation* (OGL, 2024).

Scottish Government, *A Fairer, Greener Scotland Programme for Government 2021–22* (OGL, 2021).

Scottish Law Commission, *Report on Review of Contract Law: Formation, Interpretation, Remedies for Breach, and Penalty Clauses*, March 2018 (Scot. Law Com. No.252), Appendix A.

The Report on the Tenancy of Shops (Scotland) Act 1949, (2025) Scot. Law Co. 267.

Roman Sources

Cicero, *De Officiis*, 1.33.
D.1.1.1 (Ulpianus).
Dig.1.4.2 (Ulpian).
Dig.3.5.2 (Gaius).
D.50.17.1 (Paulus).
Gaius, *Institutes*.
Justinian, *Institutes*.

Unpublished Presentations

Kenneth G.C. Reid, *Continuity and Change* (YPLF Lecture, University of Glasgow, 06 June 2019).

Roderick R.M. Paisley, *The Effect of Death in the Context of Succession* (Queen's University Belfast Seminar Paper, 10 March 2013). Accessible at https://youtu.be/7EVDRsqxHcE?t=137.

INDEX

www.ingramcontent.com/pod-product-compliance
Ingram Content Group UK Ltd.
Pitfield, Milton Keynes, MK11 3LW, UK
UKHW041832100926
8556IPUK00002B/128

9 781839 996511